THE BUS

By
John 'Sully' Sullivan

Contents

IN THE BEGINNING

Being an unsigned rock and roll band in the 1980s was radically different than it is in the 21st century. Today, an unsigned artist can record music on a computer or film a performance on a phone and publish it for the whole world to witness instantly on the internet, and you don't even need to be talented since the computer can do it all for you. But back in the day, music had to be recorded by humans who could play and sing in a recording studio, and engineers had to mix it all into a physical medium called a demo, meaning at less than professional quality. Then, the artists had to get on the road and play gig after gig, in any venue that would have them, to connect with regional audiences. Hopefully, by a million and one chance, they'd get picked up by a local radio station, and then, by a billion and one chance, get picked up by a record company that re-records the music at a much higher quality and then, the product is distributed to regional stores, and only then, could it become a top 100 hit and garner global attention.

In 1988, I had a little-known band in New York called The Dirty Rain, which by that time had only played in the tri-state area and in New England. In those days, the Northeast of the United States had become totally immersed in New Wave, pop, and electronic music, and loud rock and roll guitar bands like ours were out of fashion. But on the West Coast, more specifically, Los Angeles, it was a different story. California had again reinvented rock and roll in its own image, and bands that historically would be known as hair metal and glam rock were selling out venues with their loud guitars and drums but with a more commercial image that catered to the much-ignored female tastes of earlier hard rock bands, and The Dirty Rain felt like it wanted to crash the party. Being the leader of this particular band, it was up to me to get us there. I guess we could have flown but what fun would that be? We decided we would do what we did in the northeast: drive with all our gear and pick up gigs along the way. I was working managing a record store at the time, and between decorating window displays and dealing with customers and employees, I would call everyone I knew who could help us find a vehicle and a driver for the cross-country trip. After weeks of having every option fall through, I finished calling the last number on my list and frustratingly slammed the phone down. "Jesus!" I yelped. Unbeknownst to me, a customer shopping in the store was eavesdropping on my phone conversations.

Following my over-dramatic phone slam, he calmly uttered, "I can tell you where to get a vehicle, quick and cheap, exactly what you need." Slightly startled, I blurted, "Huh?" He grabbed a pen and a post note from the store counter and wrote down an address. He hands me the yellow paper and says, "Be there Monday through Friday, just before noon," and then turns and walks right out of the store, leaving me holding the post note. Since the internet didn't exist yet, I had to use a map to find the place. It was right off the Long Island Expressway. I had to admit I was intrigued. Back in the day, we either used the phone book or dialed 0 for the operator to find a number that matched an address, but I had no luck with either. Was I an idiot for wanting to go out there? Probably, but I was extremely desperate, and also, I also had this curious feeling. I didn't tell anyone about it because if I did, I would have never heard the end of it if it turned out to be a scam. So, on a cloudy weekday morning, excited and doubtful at the same time, I got in my beat-up 1970s Chevy Caprice Classic and made my way to the Long Island Expressway.

As I got off the exit written down on the notepad, I passed what looked like an ocean of yellow school busses as far as the eye could see, and sure enough, as I pulled onto the main street, the address on the post note was the same as the lot containing the infinite school busses. I turned and drove down a narrow driveway, bringing me to a small one-story building. I parked in front and entered the lobby. There were bells hanging from the door, which made a loud metallic clang as I opened it.

There was a thin man with greasy hair, dressed in a worn brown suit, wearing glasses, sitting at the front desk who looked up at me as I noisily entered. Mind you, at the time, I had a huge mop of curly black hair pouring over my gangly frame that was draped in ripped jeans, boots, a leather MC jacket, and black nail polish. "May I help you?" he sputtered as if he hadn't used his voice in a while. "I'm here to purchase a vehicle," I said with just a hint of false confidence. He then opened a drawer, took out a clipboard and what looked like a paddle with a number on it, and handed it to me. "Please sign in here and then go into that room and have a seat," he said, pointing to a crooked swivel door behind him. I obliged. I walked into a brightly lit room that smelled like a toxic combination of ammonia and gasoline. There was a well-worn wooden podium in the front of the room and several rows of dingy red and white colored chairs. There wasn't anyone else in there but me. I took a seat near the swivel door just in case I needed to slip out quickly and unnoticed.

After sitting alone for about 10 minutes, the same thin man from the front desk walked through those swivel doors holding a huge black ledger book. He walks up to the podium, drops the gigantic book down upon it, and opens up the pages. He turned up the volume of a grimy microphone that was clipped to a gnarled gooseneck mic holder mounted to the podium and lazily mumbled into it, "Ford F700 Blue Bird full-length school bus, starting bid, one hundred and fifty dollars, do we have anyone for $150?" In a matter of seconds, a voice inside my mind realized what was going on and started shouting within my skull. "Hey, you, yeah, you, numb nuts! You are at an auction, and they're selling an entire school bus for $150!" Stunned, I turned and looked around the empty room and then looked down at the paddle in my hand with the number on it, and my brain shouted out again "Idiot, show him the paddle!" So, I did. "We have one fifty, going, going, going, gone, Ford F700 sold for $150," said the thin man with the glasses and greasy hair. He then closed the big black book, turned off the grimy microphone, and gestured for me to follow him through the crooked, swiveled door. Back in the lobby, in a zombie-like state of mind, I signed some papers, paid the one hundred fifty dollars, and then was handed a pink slip, a receipt, and information on registration and license for driving a bus. He told me to go back out to the lot, and someone would come around to assist me. I walked back outside through the doors with the clanking bells.

After a few minutes, a young but weathered-looking dude dressed in oil-stained coveralls and smoking Marlboro reds walked up to me, looked me up and down, and says in a thick long island accent, "How ya doin, d'ya play in a band? You look like you're in a band." "I am, actually," I said. "That's what the bus is for. We're driving cross country." "Man, that's always been a dream of mine," he said with remorse. "Well, let's get you set up. Follow me." We walked around to the back of the building and that was the first time I laid eyes on The Bus. It-was-HUGE!. "Here she is," he said like a proud uncle. "My God!" I thought to myself. What the hell did I just do? I can't own this massive school bus, let alone drive one. A wave of anxiety rushed through my body. He must have seen the look on my face because he tried to encourage me. "It's gonna be great, don't worry. Have you ever driven a bus before?" he asked inquisitively. "Hell no," I sputtered. "Do you know anyone who can?" he gently pried. "Ugh, yeah, sure," I pretended. He walked me into the bus. "You won't need all these seats?" he half asked and half stated. "No, I guess not," I said, biting my lip. "I'll take a bunch out for ya, give ya some more room," he said, still trying to lift my confidence. "Come back when you have your driver, plates, and insurance, and she'll be ready to go."

Turns out there's a logical explanation for this craziness. New York state law at the time required school buses to be retired after a certain number of years so, hence the auctions. I was afraid to tell the rest of the band about the bus because I thought I'd get roasted for my gullibility, but actually, it was quite the opposite. They were taken by surprise, intrigued, excited, and, I think, impressed by my initiative. At least, that's what I told myself. Miraculously, we did know someone who could drive the bus, and he offered to come along on the trip to be our designated driver. Rick was a tall, thick, combat boot-wearing, ska punk skinhead who would take his albino pet rat with him everywhere he went. He could drink a case of Old English Malt Liquor in a single day, at which point he would then take off all his clothes in public. It was never a dull moment with Rick, but he was highly intelligent and a sweetheart and was licensed to drive trucks and, luckily, busses. Later in the week, Rick and I went to pick up the bus. With the seats removed, the inside was almost the size of a small studio apartment in Manhattan. The mechanic told us that by law, we would have to paint it a different color than yellow and recommended tinting the windows. I heard Jim Morrison's voice ringing in my head, "The Blue Bus is calling us," so blue it would become.

We decided to introduce the bus to all our friends by throwing a 'help us paint the bus party.' It was a bash. Girls with miniskirts up to their asses and dudes with hair down to their asses drank, smoked, snorted, made out, and occasionally painted. Not only did we paint the entire bus midnight blue, but the inside was graffitied, airbrushed, oiled, and sharpened into a riot of shapes, characters, graphics, poems, messages, and colors. We installed a sound system, and with the seats taken out, it sounded like a club inside. We got this adhesive style of window tinting that you cut with an Xacto knife, which surprisingly came out pretty decent. After 8 hours of partying and painting, our pedestrian yellow school bus was transformed into a metallic midnight blue mobile rock and roll assault vehicle, or did it just look like a prison bus? Either way, everyone had a blast, and we felt like a conquering army going off to war.

But let's back up in time a bit because I think it's relevant. Prior to all this, one day, while I was working at the record store, the owner came in, as he did each week, to pick up the profits that I'd put in the safe. Usually, he would go to the back of the store by himself to open the safe, but this time, he said, "Hey, take a walk with me.", so I followed him, and as he was opening the safe, he said "How would you like to be a partner in the business?" Now, he wasn't the kind of guy who had a sense of humor, at least not in the normal sense, and he wasn't necessarily the sarcastic type. So, I said, "Huh?" He said, "Yeah, All I do is come here and pick up the money; you're doing everything thing else, and besides I need to take some time off. I'll make you a partner, and then you'll be part owner of a business. It will be good for you. Think about it." Then he put the money in his bag and said, "I'll speak to you in a few days," and walked out. I was shocked. I didn't know what to say or think. I was 20 years old. I never thought about owning a business. In fact, I didn't think about anything other than playing music. I was just working at the record store to be around music all the time. Before I learned how to play instruments, I was obsessed with record albums. I didn't care about cars, clothes or sports. Whenever I would get some money, I would buy albums. I did like girls, but usually girls who also loved music. I didn't think about going to school other than studying music theory or production. The responsibility of owning a business was a disturbing proposition. I needed an adult brain to contemplate the pros and cons. I had a strange feeling like I was standing at a crossroads, and as Robert Johnson sang, "I believe I'm sinking down."

That night, after hours of lying awake in bed, I finally fell asleep. I had a terrifying dream that I was old, tired, and still working at the record store, never having traveled the world playing music. It was so real I could feel the regret and the loss. I knew in the dream something was wrong, and in it I told myself "You are dreaming, wake up!!!" Then, this giant black hole opened up, and I fell into it. I woke up in a sweat. I never had a dream like that. I got up and looked in the mirror. I was so happy that I was still young and relatively free. I knew then I wouldn't live a conventual life, but I wasn't sure that I had the talent to make it in music. I was confident I knew what good music was, but I wasn't confident that I could express it. I was afraid, and realized then that fear could keep me in the record store for the rest of my life. That same day, I had a band rehearsal.

BROTHERS IN ARMS

The Dirty Rain, like any other band, was a mix of different personalities. Mitch, the guitarist I had known the longest. We were the same age and had played in several bands together, but in past bands, I was always the drummer. In The Dirty Rain, I was the songwriter, so I relinquished the drums to be the lead singer. I always felt Mitch preferred me as a drummer, so there was a bit of tension there. I also think he was probably right; I was a much better drummer, but rock singers were hard to come by, so I took one for the team. Mitch had the rock guitarist vibe down, skinny, long hair, attitude, and he could adequately strangle a Fender Strat. Anthony, the drummer, was a few years younger and, I would say, unashamedly overweight. But he had all the rock clothes and spikey dyed black hair and matching nail polish so he was able to own it. He was also one of my drum students. I never really pursued teaching, but I would always get drummers asking me for lessons. In a way, The Dirty Rain started because Anthony wanted to play the drums on my songs.

Shane, the bass player I met when we shared a bill together, playing in opposite bands. He was a few years older, but we immediately liked each other and kept in touch. He was lanky and lean and struck the perfect bass player pose. He was also the one that got me the job at the record store. He was more of a punk rocker aesthetically, but where we all came together was with the Blues.

Mitch and Anthony were more interested in the British interpretation of the Blues but Shane and I loved the old Masters like Muddy Waters, BB King, and Lightning Hopkins. But we didn't sound like Classic or British Blues when we played. We were too loud and hyper. It was a funk-a-billy grind with a heavy metal sheen. Jack Daniels and Stimulants were needed to digest the sound. Those ingredients would become an issue eventually, but I'm getting ahead of myself. At this particular rehearsal, I wasn't at my best. I was disturbed all day by the dream the night before. Stopping for a cigarette break, we got into the same old conversation about how New York was all dance bands and Pop groups and the West Coast was where it was at. I couldn't hear it anymore, and without even realizing it, I said "What are you going to do about it?" First, there was silence, then almost in unison, they said, "What do you mean?". And I said, "Well, if you think it can't happen here, why are you still here?". Silence. Dead air. "Seriously," I said. "If you think you can't make it here, why would you stay?" Still no answer. So, I said, "It's either the truth or an excuse; either way, I'm going to find out". And that's how this whole thing started.

Now, I didn't really connect with the west coast 80s guitar rock styles. It all sounded like TV commercials and hyperbole to me. No soul. But the West Coast sound of the 60s and 70s was pure gold. Hendrix, The Doors, Jefferson Airplane, Crosby Stills, Nash and Young, The Beach Boys, Sly and the Family Stone, Santana, The Dead, and The Eagles, so many that I felt maybe there was something to that phrase, "Go west, young man, there's gold in them thar hills!" So, we had a band, a vehicle, and a driver. Now we needed some gigs. In the 21st century, you can find the promoter of a venue on a website and send them a link in an email to your website, where they can read your press and bio, look at your photos, listen to your music, and watch a video of your band in action with one click of a mouse and respond Yay or Nay instantaneously. But back in the day, you had to find out who the promoter was by six degrees of separation, put your vinyl or cassette with a printed bio and photo in an envelope, snail mail it, then hope, pray, and wait weeks, maybe months for a response. For clubs in Los Angeles back in the 1980s, the jewel of the bunch was the famous Whiskey a-Go Go on the Hollywood strip. I got the number from the phone operator, and after a few tries of calling, someone had finally picked up. Going through the chain of command I did get an address to mail our press kit and a number to call back. But in all honesty, our demo, pictures, and bio were not that impressive.

At least, I didn't think so. We weren't together very long, and the recording quality and songs were far from commercial. But we were edgy, young, and hungry, and I think that came across. Well, whatever it was, when I called back the following week, we were told we were on the schedule. We got the gig! Basically, they gave us the worst night at the worst time slot, but we didn't care. I was shocked we got anything at all. But it would be the centrifugal force that would propel us across the country. Hunter Thompson would be proud. The gig was just over a month away, so we had to get our shit together. I had a little money saved, and everyone would be chipping in for gas, tolls, repairs, and motels when needed. I decided to apply for a credit card. I didn't know anyone at the time who had a credit card. I told myself I would only use it for emergencies. More on that later.

The shopping list of a rock band about to go on the road could be an anthropological examination of the decadence of Western culture. Whiskey, Vodka, Gin, Tequila, Tabaco, Cannabis, Cocaine, Barbiturates, Amphetamine, Aspirin, Tylenol, Advil, Nyquil, Pepto-Bismol, Comtrex, Pornography, Condoms, Cookies, Cakes, Candies, and to wash it all down, Coca-Cola. Not to mention the S&M paraphernalia. Whips, chains, crops, handcuffs, gags, dog collars, blindfolds, latex, rubber, ropes, and all sorts of flavored lubricants. Also, an assortment of knives, brass knuckles, nunchakus, lead pipes, baseball bats, and a sword. The only things missing were the urns to put our ashes in when the trip was over. We also had a fair amount of gear we needed to bring. Guitars, amplifiers, speakers, mixers, microphones, stands, cables, effect pedals, drums, percussion, cymbals, hardware, and sticks. I also picked up a Roland 707 drum machine so I could make demos on the road with my 4-track cassette recorder. We decided to furnish the bus with the unimaginably filthy sofa and soiled mattress existing in our dungeon of a basement studio that would sometimes flood when it rained. Ah, the endurance and ignorance of youth. We put all the gear in the very back of the bus with the soiled mattress on top of it. We left some of the original bus seating to separate the front from the back. The disgusting sofa was quite long and took up a big chunk of the entire bus. At the time it actually seemed quite cozy, although now I would probably be repulsed.

Finally, it was time to say goodbye to our friends, girlfriends, and families. Back in the 80s, we didn't have smartphones or social media. While driving through the outback of America, we would be unreachable, disconnected, invisible, free, gone. The owner of the record store didn't even acknowledge that I didn't accept his partnership offer. He was too blown away that I actually bought a bus and would drive across the entire country with a rock band. He thought it was a stupid idea but nonetheless an exciting one. He wished us luck. It wasn't as easy separating from my girlfriend. She was super cool and understood the whole rock and roll trip, but we were very close, and I could feel her broken heart. I felt pretty shitty, but at the same time, I didn't necessarily think it was over, not for me anyway. My parents were used to me doing things they didn't understand or relate too or would never choose for themselves. They gave up a long time ago trying to have an influence on me. My sister and second oldest brother were into their own things at the time, so I don't think it phased them either way. My oldest brother was actively involved in helping with my music in any way he could. He chauffeured, parked vehicles, schlepped gear, manned security, stage managed, repaired gear, critiqued, gave advice, and ultimately, for me, was an inspiration. He was more rock and roll than any of us, and he didn't even play an instrument. He did have his own life, so he wouldn't be able to go with us, but I'm pretty sure he was getting a kick out of the whole thing.

By then, I had driven dozens of times along the entire eastern coast but never cross-country. None of us had. Without GPS or Google maps like today, it would take some time and effort to map out a route. The first challenge was to get through New York City on a forty-foot school bus. We decided to take the George Washington Bridge, which meant we had to drive through midtown Manhattan. Rick didn't flinch. After that, we would point our chariot towards Tennessee, the birthplace of rock and roll and Jack Daniels. All of us had developed a serious Jack Daniels habit, especially me, and Lynchburg seemed like a good place to stock up and see how it was made. A real slice of Americana. Since the bus couldn't go any faster than 55 mph, it would take us almost a full day to get there. Someone suggested we hit Graceland. From Tennessee, we would hit Dallas, Texas, and then across the desert to Los Angeles. Once we had a basic route, I did the research for gigs along the way. I sent tapes to venues in Nashville, Memphis, Charlotte, Atlanta, New Orleans, Dallas, Austin, and Phoenix. What the hell, the Whiskey a Go Go booked us, so why not somewhere else?

With our old lives put on hold, the day had come to hit the road. My girlfriend was with me to say goodbye and see us off. She was crying. I felt so bad. But another side of me knew that this is what being a musician was all about. You had to go on the road to connect with audiences. Back then, there was no other way. Being a musician wasn't a nine to five job or a weekly paycheck. It wasn't insurance and benefits or bonuses and raises or paid vacations and 401ks. Let's face it: musicians follow the muse, nine mythological goddesses from ancient times. It's not unlike a spiritual quest or the Knights of the Round

Table or Sufis in desert caravans. It's a belief, specifically in magic.

At least it used to be. Today, young musicians know all about social media, marketing, record deals, publishing, and merchandising. They understand that magic has nothing to do with it. It's all about getting famous and going viral. It's all about controversy, sex appeal and Likes on a social network platform. Today, people actually get famous for manipulating digital analytics by creating fake profile accounts and false hype that record companies then jump in on to create a monster snowball effect that people seem to be unable to resist. Then they make more money selling clothes and perfume than the music. Popular music today is mostly made by committees. Several composers and producers, separate from the artist, write and record the track to sound exactly like the current hit at the current moment. It's programed machines, recording and distributing machine sounds. With modern software, you can never have played a musical instrument, but you can drag, drop, copy, and paste samples like in a Word program.

Drums, guitars, keyboards, orchestras, verses, bridges, choruses, effects, and even vocals can all be created virtually and all perfectly in time and in tune. With artificial intelligence, you just have to write a prompt, and it creates the music for you. I'm not judging it; I'm just trying to convey how different it was. Music used to be raw, nasty, primal, and emotional. In other words, real! Bodies sweated, fingers bled, voices cracked, ears rang. Musicians were malnourished, sleep deprived, hungover, alcoholic, addicted, narcissistic, self-conscious, self-defeatist, manipulated, ripped off, isolated, and most of it self-inflicted because sometimes that's where the muse takes you. That's why it's Muse-Sic-k. But maybe that's too uncivilized for today's culture, who have grown up indoors, in mom and dad's house, playing video games, used to a life looking at screens. 'The Dirty Rain,' the band, was the complete opposite of all that. We knew we were raw and real, and that's all we needed to play rock and roll.

The reason all those school busses where in that lot and why they're sold so cheap is because New York State had a law that a bus could only be active in the New York educational system for a limited time. After that, they were only eligible for private use. So, as you can imagine, there was always a surplus. The plus side for us is we were able to get a vehicle quickly, cheaply, and easily. The down side is since these buses were considered almost disposable to the NY educational system, they didn't maintain them very well. We noticed pretty quickly that the bus leaked oil and transmission fluid. Also, the clutch was a bit slippery, and the brakes had to be pumped a bit. But did we care? Hell no. To us, the bus was perfect, warts and all. As we pulled away from our now-former rehearsal studio, I waved goodbye to my girl and the friends who came to see us off. There was no turning back now. It was exhilarating.

But I remember having a strange thought. My fellow band members seemed different to me at that moment, like they were the closest people in my life and complete strangers at the same time. We all upgraded our licenses so we could at least learn how to drive the bus. Since Rick was there and licensed to drive, technically so could we. We figured once we got on the open road, we would swap turns. Crazy, I know, but we didn't think anything of it; we were rolling. On a highway, maneuvering the bus was not too difficult, but on midtown Manhattan's narrow traffic-filled lanes, it was quite a bit trickier. Rick was earning his combat pay. We popped our heads out of the windows, interacting with anyone who noticed us, which was quite a few. We stuck out like a giant blue whale washed up on a public beach. Some people were cheering us on; others told us to piss off. Finally, we rolled onto the Washington Bridge. It felt like we were ancient Greeks entering the underworld and crossing over the river Styx. And in honor of Charon, instead of putting a coin in our mouths, we opened a bottle of Jack. It's an observation of mine that certain bands lean towards particular, let's say, inspirations. Some bands, primarily jam-style, reggae, or college bands, tend to smoke weed. Metal bands tend to like coke and meth.

Some hard-core bands see substances as a crutch and advocate sobriety and chanting Hare Krishna. For The Dirty Rain, alcohol was the poison of choice. Now, don't get me wrong, we indulged in anything we got our hands on, but booze was the communal sacrament. I liked to smoke a joint now and then because it didn't make me tired like it might for some people. The other guys liked it more in mellower situations. Mitch was more of a "Let's do some lines" kind of guy. That wasn't my favorite thing. I never thought the comedown or the hangover was worth it. Shane liked to mix in some pills. I could hang with that if they were downs, but Speed did the same thing to me as Coke. And Anthony, I think, got the highest off of fast food, a true American. But one thing is for sure: once we got enough booze in us, we indulged in anything and everything. I'm not quite sure why that was; perhaps it made it easier to be perceived as someone else.

It's so hard to be recognized as a real rocker when no one knows who you are, so you leverage your behavior as a way to prove your authenticity, a cultural leftover from the 60s perhaps, or maybe it's more primal than that. We really were four very different personalities, and the drugs and strong drink initiated us into our own little secret society, or maybe even simpler still, pardon the cliché, we were just bad boys. It was precarious, anti-social, illegal, abusive, and, most of all, necessary. It made throwing your whole life away to join the circus seem like the most practical choice, and we were good at it too.

We managed not to be sober seven days a week and still managed to avoid incarceration, unemployment, and homelessness, although in the past, that wasn't always the case, and this story is just beginning, but like they say, practice makes perfect. The point I'm trying to make with these details is that there was nary a time that the former public-school bus, now converted rock and roll mothership, was ever piloted by a sober sailor. By that point, it was the only way possible for us to function. But, of course, that is by no means sustainable. But once again, I get ahead of myself.

GO WEST, YOUNG MAN

For anyone who has past the threshold of Manhattan into New Jersey knows the roadside cultural desert of industrial factories, refineries, and chemical stench that permeates the once abundant life teaming swampland. Strips of car sales lots, corporate fast-food joints, and billboard signs stretch far out into the hazy horizon. As a New Yorker, you can almost feel bad for New Jersey, guilty even, for casting such a dark and heavy shadow over an otherwise passionate noble State. Unlike New York, Jersey still had somewhat of a rock scene, although nothing compared to its 60s and 70s heyday. But there was something about the Jersey spirit that resonated with what was happening on the West Coast. Or maybe it was just the affinity for hairspray. Anyway, as Jersey evaporated into our rear-view mirror, the spurs of alienation dug into our psychology. This can happen to New Yorkers when they travel through other states. Not necessarily other countries, more so other states. It has something to do with cultural elitism that's a byproduct of immigrant culture. We're not Hicks, Rednecks, or Cowboys, as if those are somehow sub-par cultures. As New Yorkers, we consider ourselves educated, diverse, sexually liberated, atheist progressives and have convinced ourselves we are better than the other 49 States because we know the difference between coffee and an Americano. I get it that if you tried to order a Penne Ragu in the Midwest in the 80s, you would have gotten egg noodles, ketchup, and hamburger meat, but that's no excuse to vilify an entire country. New Yorkers just didn't have an exotic enough pallet for slow-cooked whole hog BBQ or Gumbo and Dirty Rice. Not yet, anyway.

But the one Indigenous culinary accouterment we did indulge in was Jack Daniels. Jack is not a bourbon, as it is sometimes misrepresented. Neither is it a scotch or single malt. Technically, it is a Tennessee whiskey, corn mash specifically, and ultimately the quickest way to go from sober to nerve-numbing drunkenness with just a few hard swigs. Although considered a 'Sipping Whiskey," after a while, one does build a tolerance to it and must resort to drinking it right from the bottle and thus became our preferred means of delivery. Opening a bottle of Jack between us meant that we were all making a commitment to rock and roll in every situation that was about to come our way. It meant throwing away any self-consciousness and saying the first thing that came to your head. It meant casually and constantly interacting with total strangers. It meant performing daring feats of physical stupidity. It meant a constant pace of one-upmanship that guaranteed Olympian bouts of absurdity and obscenity. And damn if it didn't make everything gut-wrenching hilarious. We needed Jack. It greased the wheels so that our rock could roll. Jack so numbed reality that the stench and filth of rock clubs, roadside motels, dirty tour buses, and our own compromised hygiene were tolerable or that blown speakers and deaf sound engineers hardly mattered. Or that you were actually interested in what the girl you were hitting on or was hitting on you, was saying. It also had a practical application. Spending the pittance that American rock clubs paid bands on buying booze at the bar was financially unsound. So, we'd either smuggle a bottle or two into the dressing room or have our own flasks tucked into our clothes. Back in the day, getting cases of the stuff at discount prices wasn't so easy. So, we decided to go straight to the source. Lynchburg, Tennessee, would be our first destination. We thought of it as a wise business investment.

On the way to Lynchburg, we'd passed by the great eastern seaboard cities of Philly, Baltimore, and D.C., Places we've all played before in different bands. It didn't make sense why we chose not to book any shows in any of those towns. I believe the sentiment was to get away from the northeast as fast as possible. Out of those three, Baltimore had the closest to some kind of rock scene. D.C. still had some A-Go-Go funk going down, but like the other two, you got the feeling that better days had come and gone. Perhaps it was better to keep our hopes up and strive for greener pastures. We drove pretty much a full day, stopping at gas stations, small-town convenience stores, or anywhere we thought might be a view of some kind. I'm pretty sure Rick may have indulged in some chemical enhancements because he was pretty hyper and was speaking in rapid-fire bursts. We all took turns driving, but he did the bulk of it. We had already killed one bottle of Jack and even opened up another. We drove all through the night. Either we were too excited, or for some of us, too stimulated to fall asleep. Also, too wasted to deal with a motel. We ended up arriving at the parking lot of the Jack Daniel's Distillery at six in the morning.

Nobody was there but the birds and the crickets. It probably would be hours till anyone showed up. So, we set up camp, blasted music, and kept drinking. After a few hours, a car pulled into the lot. It seemed to us like it abruptly slowed down as if it was surprised and concerned by our presence. Then, it turned and went to park on the opposite side of the lot. Then another car pulled in, in a similar fashion and then parked next to the first one. The occupants got out of their vehicles and indiscreetly stared in our direction. I'm sure we were a sight to behold. A giant blue whale of a bus with tinted windows blasting Chicago blues early in the morning and five mangy-looking young men, four with straggly hair falling down their backs and holes in their jeans, and one completely bald giant. They just stood there staring. So, we stared back. Normally, in situations like this is when Rick would take all his clothes off, which pretty much scared anyone away who may have contemplated, if even for a brief moment, of being 'the good citizen' by reminding us that "This is private property" or asking "Do you belong here?" One look at Rick and that potential good citizen ran off to fight another day.

But our good luck held out, and Rick kept his clothes on because another car pulled into the lot and joined up with the other two. Now, there were three of them and five of us. Finally, one of them started to walk in our direction. He was a round feller with a beard, a trucker hat, and construction boots. He got about thirty feet from us, then stopped and said in a deep southern drawl, "Can I help yoooo!?" I slurred back, "Yyyo brother, we're a band ffffrom New York City, and we drove all the wwwway here to watch you make Jack Daniels!". The rest of the boys busted out laughing, and the round dude with the trucker hat splayed a huge grin and rocked back and forth on his construction boots, and said, "Well damn, y'all getting an early start! Tours don't begin for a while yet, but you're more than welcome to visit the gift shop." He then spun around on his boots and started walking back to the others on the opposite side of the parking lot shaking his head with the trucker hat on it and chuckling to himself.

Inside the main building was a kind of museum, slash gift shop, slash liquor distributor, with hundreds of cases stacked up and filled with every style of Jack Daniels you could imagine. There were versions that were only distributed to the southern states that you couldn't get up north or limited editions that were only sold in Tennessee or just at the distillery. Also, there were all kinds of drinks that were flavored with Jack. It was a drunkard's dream if I ever did see one. After a while, other customers began strolling in, and eventually, another portly fellow with a beard wearing a JD T-shirt and hat, made an announcement. "If you are taking the tour, please follow me," and so we did. He took us and a few other tourists to a room beside the gift shop and introduced himself. He told us he was our guide and that the tour would last about an hour and a half. But first, he invited us to watch a short video documentary of the Jack Daniels story, and then after that he directed us to go outside and get on the distillery's tour bus. The other tourists stayed for the film, but we were too wasted and distracted, so we went outside to smoke cigarettes instead. Eventually, the tourists came outside and were getting on the bus. We stamped out our butts and then joined them. The difference in how we looked compared to everyone else on the bus was polarizing. Us, in our skin-tight, ripped, and torn black jeans, and violence and drug-imaged band t-shirts and tattoos, while adorning ear, nose, and tongue rings, and long, very long, dyed black, blond and silver manic panic hair, and them, in their bright-colored polo shirts and bleach white tennis shoes, socks, and shorts, sporting bushy bun hairdos and crew cuts.

We must have looked like aliens from another planet. Remember, this is the 80s, but as we got on the bus, they were all smiling. And we smiled back. You got the feeling everyone was talking about us. The driver got on the bus and took his seat, and the tour guide stood up front to address our group. They both turned to each other, waving their hands in front of their faces. "God damn, it smells like a distillery in here," said the driver. The guide said, "Seems some people figured out a way to bypass the Lynchburg 'Dry Town' laws." "Dry town laws?" asked Shane. "Yip," said the guide. "Lynchburg ain't got a single bar or liquor store. It's illegal to sell any hooch. An act of self-preservation, leftover from prohibition. But don't worry y'all, we'll do plenty of sampling after the tour." Something to look forward too.

I found the whole process of making Jack Daniel's Tennessee Whiskey quite interesting. So interesting that I felt it sobered me up. I've always found the fermentation process captivating. It's a popular theory that fermenting grain was the inspiration for civilization. Nomadic tribes returning seasonally to familiar locations discovered that rainwater inside leftover grain vessels had transmuted into the food of the gods. Fermentation requires the concept of time. The transformation of yeast into alcohol sterilizes water, allowing communities to stay longer in particular locations, eventually leading to farming, domestication, language, writing, and religion. The keepers of this magic knowledge became the high priests or the ministers of culture or, more specifically, a cult or occult. Hidden underneath everything is the alchemic ritual of culture. Like T-Rex said, "Just like Rock and Roll." Think of rock and roll as a hundred-proof cocktail. One-part Irish jig, one-part Italian tarantella, one-part indigenous ceremonial song, marinated in African voodoo and boiled together into a Delta Blues gumbo by a Creole chef, then amplified to eleven by Nicola Tesla, Les Paul, and Muddy Waters. These were our rock and roll ancestors. Our legions, our religion. We're all ministers of culture in an ancient cult called civilization. And rock and roll are the noun and verb description of our celestial home. Maybe I wasn't sober yet. We spent most of the day at the distillery. We sampled specialty batches, ate food, purchased a case of Old No.7 and a case of Gentleman Jack, and they gave us a box full of mini-inflight single-serving bottles on the house. Shane convinced them to sell him half an aging barrel because he loved the wood engraving on it. We literally had to reconfigure all the gear and the mattress to get it on the bus. We also made some new friends. Everyone was enamored by our big blue bus and our journey to the left coast. One guy told us we should head to Memphis next. He said he had a friend who managed a new live music club there and that he would tell him we were coming. That sounded good to us. Eventually, it was closing time, and we'd already been awake and partying for two days. The JD crew said that it was fine if we slept it off in their parking lot and that they would let the local sheriff know we had permission. I believe we were all pleased with ourselves and each other. Seemed like our journey was off to a good start.

Sleeping on the bus presented many challenges. Basically, we could only lay flat on the couch and the mattress. If we all crashed at the same time that meant two of us had to sleep sitting up. With an abundance of sleep deprivation and drugs and alcohol, that usually wasn't too much of a problem, but eventually, we would learn to take turns. Upon waking that morning, our next issue was hygiene. We stunk! So far none of us had bathed, brushed, or changed our clothes since we left. We had a big yellow water cooler with a red screw top that we ended up using more as a sink and shower than for drinking. We propped the cooler on the first step of the bus entrance and lined up in front of it with our towels and toothbrushes like soldiers in trenches on the front line. Eventually, it became a routine, but that first morning, it was a bizarre sight. We would also realize that it wasn't the best place for the cooler because it created a mud puddle in front of the bus entrance. After that it was off to the bushes with our toilet paper rolls.

Oh, the humanity. Needless to say, all this humility had a bonding effect on us. Ultimately, the way we originally came together was more of a process of elimination than a curated casting call. Playing in rock bands can quickly divide the weekend warriors from the hardcore believers. Most of the musicians we knew started to move on, doing weddings and supper club jazz or cover bands while hanging on to their day jobs. Some went off to college, while others got married and had babies. But we weren't ready to give up. Not yet, anyway. I don't think we thought we'd be famous big stars or anything. We just wanted to be in proximity to it. There'd be plenty of time for weddings, jobs, and babies later.

After we all took practice runs driving the bus around the parking lot, we mapped a route to Memphis. Named after the ancient capital of Egypt, Memphis, USA, was the birthplace of rock and roll, the bastard child of blues and country western. Some people say the term 'rock and roll' is a euphemism for sex. As a musician you'd know that 'rock' and 'roll' are words used to describe musical dynamics. Like when you rock a piano, it simply means your fingers rock back and forth between two notes, usually with the left hand on the bass keys. And then, to create a counterpoint rhythmic tension, you roll the fingers of the right hand creating a frantic trill on the high notes. Put 'em together, and you got rock and roll. Eventually, the contrabass, and later still, the electric bass copied the piano's left hand, and the guitar copied the piano's right hand, and the drummer landed somewhere in the middle, swinging between the two. These are the basic ingredients of rock and roll music. You can change the instruments, the melodies, the harmony, the arrangements but that groove created by the rhythmic tension is key. Rock and roll did not start out as popular music. Nor did it intend to be. It was meant to be rebellious, subversive, counter-cultural, sexual, and most of all, Cool Daddy O! After the whole world went to war with itself for a second time in the 1940s, it went on pause to create nuclear weapons with the idea that the third time would be the final encore. Americans, especially teenagers, weren't having it. Throw in the huge profits American companies made from rebuilding bombed-out Europe and Japan with the increase in middle-class earnings and you had the perfect recipe for a generation gap. Young people in the 1950s now had access to things only available in the military just a decade earlier. They had more choices, more freedoms, more culture. Business people saw a massive new market emerging, and everyone was looking to strike gold. One of those business people was Sam Philips. Philips started a record company in 1952 and called it Sun Records. The sun-worshiping Egyptians would have approved. He rented a small space at 706 Union Ave., Memphis, Tennessee. He recorded everything from gospel, blues, hillbilly, country, boogie, and western swing. In 1953, Elvis Presley walked through the door, and the rest is history. After that, there was Johnny Cash, Jerry Lee Lewis, Carl Perkins, and Roy Orbison just to name a few. Memphis, and especially Sun Records, became a new musical mecca. The studio is still operating today. We added that to our 'to-do' list and started the five-hour drive to the birthplace of rock and roll.

The bus was slow. It topped out at 55 mph, and you could hear and feel the motor struggling at that speed. We usually hovered at around 50 mph. We had every window opened since there was no air conditioner, and the Tennessee afternoon heat was starting to sizzle. I made a makeshift turban out of one of my shirts to keep the curly mane of locks off my shoulders and back. Man, that bus really rattled. It was like being in a giant tin can that was rolling down a mountain. We had to blast the stereo just to hear the music. What a din. And we were all feeling a little queasy from the day before. We basically were pulling over almost every hour. Partly because we needed a break from the noise, and partly because sometimes we would switch drivers, but mostly because we were kind of bored. It was hard to have a nuanced conversation or hear yourself practice. Even reading was difficult because the bus shook so much. So, against our better judgment, we would start to party again, and that led to wanting to release excess energy. If we saw a store or a street that looked interesting, we wanted to investigate. Any excuse to buy roadside crap.

When we entered a truck stop, we were like an invading army. First of all, this big blue rattling bus pulls in, blasting music, and then five disheveled, obviously out-of-place, long-haired individuals step out, drinking beer, smoking cigarettes, and wearing sunglasses and turbans. It's wasn't a pretty sight. Once inside the store, we would all spread out to our favorite sections. I would look for magazines, Mitch for sandwiches, Anthony for sweets, and Shane and Rick for beer. Usually, the cheapest beer tended to be Rolling Rock or PBR. When funds were really low, they'd be known to indulge in malt liquor. It was hard for store owners to keep their eyes on all of us. This is when we also started to pocket certain items. We would pay for stuff, but we would also not pay for stuff. It became a game. We would compete with each other or team up and help each other with a distraction. It was all just junk food or crappy products, but it was getting away with it that was exhilarating or at least placated the boredom for a while.

Memphis, besides New York, was the first time on the trip we had to deal with the logistics of maneuvering and parking the bus in a city. It wasn't easy. There were a few close calls. The famous Beale Street was blocked off for vehicles, but paid parking was pretty cheap. It took a while to find a lot that had room for us, but we managed to find one. It was a relief having the bus parked. We could stretch our legs and be free for a while. Beale Street was hopping. People everywhere. Tons of food and booze are being sold on the street. You could hear the live music coming out of the bars. The first items we bought were corn dogs and beer, and then we strolled around the four or five blocks that were the entertainment district. We came across one place that had a sign outside saying, "Tonight, Albert King." I couldn't believe it. I rushed right in for more details. The door guy said there was a cover charge and to sit at a table there'd be a food and drink minimum. I didn't hesitate. "I'll take a table. I said," "as close as possible." Albert King was one-third of the Blues triple dynasty of BB King, Freddie King, and Albert King. He played a Gibson Flying V left-handed, strung for a righty, meaning he played the guitar upside down. He had a smooth voice and a laid-back demeanor. Shane, being a fan, was just as excited as I was. Rick was totally up for anything. Mitch and Anthony seemed more concerned with the cover charge and table minimum but eventually decided to join in.

We got a table pretty damn close. We ordered drinks and food. I remember the audience being much older than us. I believe we were the youngest ones there. That is probably one of the reasons Mitch and Anthony were reluctant to go in. I never needed to relate to an artist personally if they made music I liked. If it felt good and moved my soul, it didn't matter what age, sex, race, or ideology the artist had. But I also realized that's not the case for everyone. Mitch and Anthony were very concerned with Identifying with what was considered hip and contemporary. Rick was very involved with the Ska community, which had a fashion uniform and strong social elements to it. Shane's roots were in punk, but as he got older, he found a love of roots music, and that's where he and I connected. I never got into music because it was cool or fashionable. I was obsessed with music before I knew what cool or fashion was. And not just any music. Blues music. One of my earliest memories was when I was around 3 years old; I was in the supermarket with my mom. She would place me in the top of the shopping cart where they used to have a makeshift chair for kids, and I would get rolled around in it. Since this was during the wild sixties, it wasn't unusual for her to leave me in an aisle for a minute or two to grab some items close by, but I didn't even notice. I was more curious about the sound of the music coming out from the ceiling speakers. They were at just the right volume, where you could hear everything clearly but not so loud to over-power the natural reverb of the space, creating this almost meditative ambiance that pulled me in. Then, every once in a while, an echoey voice would interrupt the music with an in-store announcement.

I was captivated by this experience. I was listening deeply. On one particular shopping spree, as my mom stepped away, I heard this music that resonated with me. It was my first Déjà vu because I recognized it. I recognized in it the tone, the rhythm, and the pain. It wasn't like the usual music playing in the store, and I immediately connected to it. I could hear clearly the way the harmony of the root tone was changing and then returning back and forth.

And how the voice repeated the same thing over the tonal changes. Even before I heard it through the speakers, I knew the progression would change a third time, then return to the second change, and then finally back to the root. And that's exactly what happened. It was like I woke up in a dream. I knew I was a baby, but I also knew I was here (hear) before. The sequence I was hearing was literally the Blues chord progression. In Western musical terms, it's called a One Four Five, represented by Roman numerals. I, IV, V, are the distance in intervals or pitch of the chords in a progression, one being the root chord or key, four being four tones away in the scale of the key, and five being five steps away, sometimes called a turnaround because it brings you back to the start of the progression. Now, these intervals are used in all kinds of music. But blues has a specific 'call and answer' structure usually in 8, 12, or 16 bars or measures of time. I could 'see' this structure in my head, and from that day, I was on a grail quest for the Holy Blues.

Eventually, I found it, first in my older brothers Jimi Hendrix and Johnny Winter albums, but eventually, I discovered Muddy Waters, Lightning Hopkins, Etta James, Son House, John Lee Hooker, Bessie Smith, and Robert Johnson. But this passion wasn't something I was able to share. Everyone I knew thought this music was too rootsy, too raw, too old. Admittedly, the recordings were mostly low-fi, but to me, that only added to the vibe. And these artists were from a bygone era, with too many skeletons in the closet and out-of-date clothes and hairstyles. Again, for me, that deepened the feeling. Traditional Blues wasn't popular in young culture in 1980s America. New Wave and Rap were the cutting edge. Drum machines, synthesizers, and ADAT digital recording and digital effects were all the rage. Live music was out, and MTV was in. DJs became superstars, and Rock became Classical. It was Thomas Sowell, the brilliant economist, who said, "Each new generation born is in effect an invasion of civilization by little barbarians, who must be civilized before it is too late."

The music business, not known for its loyalty, saw an opportunity to civilize the growing rap and electronic music scene, which didn't have the enormous overhead of live musicians, recording studios, and elaborate stage productions. New music meant new business models, and if you weren't hip, you weren't paid. So, it's not surprising young people avoided roots music and styles. Unless, of course, it was sampled. They were afraid of being irrelevant. To its credit, the West Coast rock scene was still dreaming of platinum albums and sold-out stadiums, even though the writing was on the wall.

When Albert King took the stage, the whole place rose up in their seats for a standing ovation. He was a big man dressed in a fine suit. You could tell the years have been hard on him. He was old. He snapped a tempo with his fingers, kicking his backing group into a chill shuffle groove. He introduced himself and the band, then slipped into a slow blues. Right off the bat, those signature string bends seared straight into my bones. That's what detractors of the blues don't understand. Blues is primarily a vocal music. Even if it's not a human voice, you sing blues with your instrument. When guitar heroes emulate their blues masters, they're trying to make the guitar sing like a human voice. That's the reason for all the excruciating pain faces. Bending those wire stings with your fingers is painful. It's not a pose or an act. It's just as much a physical expression as a musical one. As the slow blues builds into a crescendo, Albert reaches higher and higher on the strings as if to say, "Here I am, God. Take me!" and then, SNAP! A string breaks! The whole place groans as if we all broke with it. But without missing a beat, a big smile comes over his face, as if he accomplished what he set out to do. He meant to break that string. I learned a great lesson at that moment. The band fell back down to the chill-out shuffle.

Albert walks up to the mic, pulls a string right out of his suit pocket, and starts telling a story about how he made his first guitar out of a cigar box down in Mississippi. All the while restringing the guitar and tuning it as he spoke. You knew he had done this a thousand times. Like he could do it in his sleep. That was the second great lesson I learned, and this damn show just started.

Mr. King hung around after the gig to greet people, sign autographs and I got to shake his hand. I could see in his eyes he was tired or not feeling well. I didn't want to pressure him, so I left it at just a handshake and a thank you. We headed back out onto the street, where there was still plenty of action going on. We again got pretty buzzed and still had the energy to burn. We figured we'd stroll around awhile to see if we could get lost. Once we got away from Beale Street, we came across a strip club with bright lights and a big sign saying 'Gentleman's Club' and 'Live Girls.' Both Mitch and Anthony were now the ones rushing to get inside. By that time, I had been to a few so-called 'Clubs' down in Miami. That's just what people seem to do in Miami. But it's not my go to for a night out, but when in Rome. At the entrance of this club stood the biggest dude I've ever seen. His arm was wider than my entire body. He had a baby face like he was maybe 25, but his cold, dead eyes looked like they had seen it all. He scowled at us and then, with a growl, asked us for IDs. He actually seemed to study them, looking for anything suspicious. Then, looking away from us, he handed the IDs back and waved us in. That was intimidating, we thought.

Inside the club, the music was loud. A giant bar encircled a stage with a pole in the center and a topless dancer in a thong attached to it like a ballerina doll to a music box. Trucker dudes were sitting on chairs in front of the stage, waving dollars at the twirling dancer. What took me by surprise was how excited some of the girls working there were to see us. It was like we were the Beatles or something. A few of them were actually quite hot-looking. They brought us over to a table near the back and sat down with us. A waitress came over, and we ordered some drinks. We were asked all kinds of questions. Where were we from? What were we doing there? Were we in a band? One of the cute girls was running her fingers through my hair, shaking her head and smiling. "I just love your curls," she said in a sweet tea drawl that'd hurt your teeth. She had a great body and barely anything on it except for high heels and tiny spandex shorts. I looked at her face and guessed she must have been about 18. It was weird but we were looking into each other's eyes and smiling like we were sharing a long-lost feeling. Some of the girls had to go and dance their set, and the rest of the boys got up to mingle. My new friend grabbed me by the hand and said, "Come with me!" She dragged me through a door that had a sign that read 'Stop. Employees Only.' But the curve of her butt shut off the part of my brain that critically thinks, and so I followed. We walked through what looked like the inside of a closet. We pushed through a sea of robes, dresses, feathers, sequins, fishnets, and polyester.

Eventually, we came to a small dressing room with some folding tables, chairs, and mirrors on the walls. There was another dancer in there taking off her street clothes. As we entered the room, she smiled and looked at me and said, "Well, hello, welcome to the spider's web." I was lost for words, so I just waved at her. Still not knowing my new friend's name, she reached into her skin-tight spandex shorts and produced a little clear plastic bag filled with white powder. She then scooped her sparkly red painted pinky nail into the magic dust and brought it up to my nostrils. Not being a novice or a germaphobe, I leaned into her finger and snorted. The other dancer, now equally undressed, came over and said, "My turn," and inhaled a nail-full. All three of us finished the little bag of white powder, and then, out of nowhere, we just started kissing. All three of us, licking and sucking each other's faces like fish in a bowl. I was grabbing every part of them that I could get my hands on, and so were they. I distinctly remember thinking, "This has got to be a dream; it's just too good."

And then a sharp pain went through my entire body. "What the hell is happening to me?" I thought. It took me a few seconds to realize I was being lifted off the ground by my hair! I could hear the girls screaming, but I couldn't see because my eyes were rolling into the back of my head. I tried to disengage whatever was scalping me and I felt a giant fist locked onto my curly locks. I realized then it was the bouncer from the front door. He literally carried me off the ground, from my hair, through the dressing room, through the closet, through the door with the 'Stop. Employees Only' sign, using my head as a battering ram, through the entire club for everyone to see, to the entrance where we showed our IDs, and then grabbed the back of my ripped black jeans and tossed me into the air like a sandbag off the back of a truck.

I landed right on my face inside a cloud of dust. I rolled over, coughing and spitting blood, whereupon opening my eyes, I found I was staring down the barrel of a gun pointed at my face. The soul-numbing shock of fear froze me like a marble statue. 'Sweet Jesus.' I thought, 'I'm about to die.' and closed my eyes. "If I ever see you round here again, I'm gonna kill you," said the mammoth bouncer in the voice of Satan himself. After pointing the gun at me for what felt like an eternity, he put it back in his pocket, turned, and went back into the club. By that time, half the customers and dancers were outside, wondering if they were going to witness an execution. The truckers were laughing their asses off and patting each other on the back. The girls seemed genuinely shaken up, and so did my band. They slowly came towards me as if they saw a ghost. They quickly helped me up. "Can you walk?" asked Shane. I nodded. "Then let's get the fuck out of here. Now!" cried Mitch. Shane and Rick half-carried me as I gained my footing. We headed back to the bus. In a few minutes I was feeling much better. My lip was cut, and my body was a little sore.

What really hurt was my scalp. I believe there was some kind of internal damage. But I kept it to myself. They all wanted to know what happened. I told them the story with the two girls in the dressing room and the coke and the making out. Their eyes and mouths were wide open. When we got to the lot, we ended up paying for another day of parking. When the cashier wasn't looking, we snuck into the lot in between parked cars and quietly got on the bus. I collapsed on the couch. "Fuck, we thought you were dead," said Anthony. "Me too," I confessed. And then, after a moment of silence and a few heavy exhales of a cigarette, Mike asked "Was it worth it?" I tilted my head and thought for a moment and said, "I do believe it was," and we all busted out laughing, not necessarily because it was funny, but because it was a relief. But damn, my scalp hurt.

The next morning, I was sore all over. I sat in the driver's seat of the bus. The rear-view mirror was huge, and you could see your whole body in it. It was the only mirror we had. I looked like shit. My lip was swollen, and I had scratches all over my face. I wasn't sure, but I thought underneath the hair of my scalp was black and blue. Then, the image of those two girls popped into my head, and I tried to push that thought away. Everyone seemed relieved that I was relatively ok. Everyone wanted breakfast and a restroom, so we decided to head out. Shane mentioned that we were right by the Mississippi River, so we made a little detour. Considered the "Nile of North America," the river was the reason the city was named Memphis. It was the main artery that pumped Blues, Jazz, and Rock and Roll into the heart of the country. From the Mississippi Delta to the City of Chicago, the blues flowed from country folk to city slickers. The five of us stood on the bank and silently stared at the beautifully calm river. There was no one there but us. It was quite relaxing. The Tennessee heat was beginning to flare up. Then Shane said, "You know, it's a blues tradition to be Baptized in the Mississippi River."

Of course, he looks over at me and raises his eyebrows. I look back with a smile, and we both start taking our shoes off. "Noooo," says Anthony. "You two are crazy," said Mitch. "They're gonna do it." Said Rick. Shane and I stripped down to our skivvies and tipped-toed our way into the muddy waters. It was exhilarating. I really did feel I was being baptized. Sean had a big smile on his face. The other three were laughing and freaking out at the same time. There was a slight current that got exponentially stronger the further from the shore we went. Not wanting to push my luck, I decided swimming around like it was a pool took away from the ceremonial vibe, so I got out. Sean stayed in a bit longer. It felt really good, actually. We dried off in the sun and got dressed. It probably was a bit of adrenalin, but I did feel different. Like the night before was a baptism by fire, and this morning a baptism by water. One thing was for sure: we were having a blast. We headed back to town for a much-needed breakfast of eggs and grits at a diner. Shane, again, was the man with the Itinerary. We should go to Sun Records studio today. Sounded good to me.

LONG LIVE ROCK AND ROLL

In 1953, a young man named Elvis Presley walked into Sun Studios in Memphis, Tennessee. And for three dollars, he recorded a song to give his mom for her birthday. Not long after, Sun Studios became known for the sound of rock and roll. It's quite humbling when you walk into this minuscule, drab studio and realize how many incredible and historical recordings were made in that unassuming room. It still was a working studio after hours, and we could actually book studio time if we wanted, but the engineer wasn't there, so we were told to either call or come back later. We added that idea to our flexible itinerary. Since there wasn't anyone else in the studio, they let us just hang out and take in the vibes. I brought a bunch of harps with me, meaning harmonicas, because you never know if a jam will start up somewhere. I had only begun playing harp about a year earlier.

A friend of mine bought one and didn't understand why he couldn't make it sound like anything other than a campfire song or a bad Bob Dylan impersonation. I asked to try, and as soon as I started to play, he said, "Hey. How'd you do that?" "Do what?" I replied. "Make those notes bend," he said, slightly frustrated. I said I didn't know. He grabbed the harp back and tried again. There was that cowboy campfire sound. He handed it back to me, and this time, I really got into it. Now, I'm not saying I was any good, but it sounded like the blues when I played it. It was a mystery to both of us. I later learned that he was playing 'Harmonica' and I was playing 'Harp.' The Harmonica was developed in Europe in the early 19th century. Used primarily to play European folk songs, it became popular quite quickly. It eventually made its way to the Americas, but in America it was played quite differently than the European style. To play the harmonica over Blues or Ragtime a technique known as cross key was used. That meant the player emphasized different notes than the key the instrument was tuned for.

Inside every musical scale are other scales, or modes, that a musician can lean more into and change a feeling or emotion. Dexterity or difficulty with modes depends on one's ear. You have to be able to hear the cross key in your head clearly while you're playing in the assigned key. Probably because I'd listened to so much blues by that point, my ear naturally was drawn to the cross keys. I was playing Harp, slang for harmonica. Sun Studio had a small drum kit and piano in the live room and a couple of badly neglected Acoustic guitars. I started to blow on the harp, and very discretely, the boys commandeered the other instruments. At first, we just played a quiet, slow blues. We were surprised no one came in to stop us. A strange feeling came over me. I suddenly felt I was caught up in the current of history. Inside that studio, time and space seemed to disappear, like somehow, I was there before and I wondered, was I stuck in the past? Or was rock and roll a ghost that haunted my thoughts and memory? It was then that I realized that from this tiny recording studio, the whole world changed. I also noticed that the little jam we were having had gotten much louder and rambunctious. That's when the studio door opened, and we were politely asked to leave the premises.

We still had some day left before the night kicked in. We wanted to track down the manager of that club, the guy mentioned at the Jack Daniel's distillery. Again, Shane was the man with the Plan. "Let's do Graceland," he announced, and we all agreed. In honor of the great rock and roll movie 'Spinal Tap' we mimicked the scene where the band stands in front of Elvis' grave and sings in very bad cockney harmony, "Since my baby left me, I found a new place to dwell!". But first, we needed to get back to the bus for some inspiration. When we returned to the lot, we learned from one of the employees that Graceland was too far of a walk, but there were shuttles and cabs that got you there pretty quickly. We popped into the blue bus for a few swigs and puffs and then headed out to flag us a ride.

Like the military, the early days of rock and roll, except for a few outliers, were predominantly a man's game. An expression of liberated masculinity celebrated by predominately young, ecstatic females. Chuck Berry, Bo Diddley, Jerry Lee Lewis, Carl Perkins, and, for a little while, Little Richard all forged an image of the Bad Boy breaking all the institutional rules. But Elvis' image was different. He made it known he loved his Mama. He portrayed pride when he was drafted into the army. He played the television and Hollywood game by softening his image. It almost seemed as if he went out of his way to portray that he was the Good Boy. In essence, he turned all the energy and angst of rock and roll onto himself. The more famous he got, the more accepted he became, the more self-destructive he behaved. This would become a pattern that would continue with future Rock Stars. I was shocked at how accessible those famous front gates of Graceland were to the main road, almost like he wanted all of Memphis to see the hillbilly had done good. Also surprising was how unassuming the main house was. For the King of Rock and Roll and one of the most famous people that has ever lived, it was quite quaint. We bought tickets at the ticket office and walked into the house with a crowd of other tourists. We were a few days on a bender by this point and seemed to be struggling with proper civilized etiquette. The other tourists seemed so serious. It was moments like these that made it irresistible for us not to turn into clowns.

The first act of our clowning repertoire was to start a farting contest as we walked from room to room. As the tourists did their best to keep their distance, we were too busy falling down laughing to even pay attention to the tour going on. There were chandeliers, shag rugs, fireplaces, plastic-covered furniture, multiple TV sets and stereos, gold and platinum records on the wall, mirrored staircases, porcelain monkey statues, a jungle room, a piano room, a recreation room with a bar, his famous jumpsuits ensconced in glass. But we were too busy terrorizing the tourists to take it all in. At one point we all fell into a laughing frenzy that was uncontrollable. When one of us would finally stop laughing, somebody else would fart at the precise moment, starting the whole cycle over again.

Extremely immature, I know, but the comedic timing of the farts was admittedly quite impressive. It's hard to explain, but for some reason, the whole feeling of going through this person's house as if it was a ride in Disneyland just seemed ludicrous to us, like they were still milking the fame that eventually drowned Elvis. I felt he was right there with us, laughing at the ridiculousness of it all. Finally, we ventured outside. There were cars, motorcycles, golf carts, the famous Pink Cadillac, and a meditation garden with a fountain. Interesting, I thought. We made our way towards the garden and began to gain some composure. We circled around the fountain, and right there was Elvis' grave. It took me and the boys totally by surprise. We had no idea he was buried right there, and it was startling. Then, out of nowhere, a shrill scream exploded out of a woman tourist's mouth as she collapsed in front of Elvis' grave. Her companion bent down to absorb and console her. Then another, and then another did the same. All of these middle-aged and senior-aged women collapsed in tears at the site of Elvis' grave. It was bizarre and mortifying. Now we really were in the Spinal Tap movie. Too much fucking perspective. "Let's get the hell out of here."

Heading back to the bus, we were hungry, dirty, and tired. We paid for another day's parking and took note that we were not being thrifty with our expenses. Next on our to-do list was to check out that club we learned about at the distillery. Not everyone was into going. I felt obligated since I was the one attempting to book the gigs. Rick and Shane accompanied me, I believe, in the hope of avoiding a potential repeat of what happened at the strip club. Anthony and Mitch tentatively agreed to catch up with us later.

In the late 80's, Beale Street was experiencing the beginning of a renaissance. The '60s and '70s were hard times financially for downtown Memphis. Many people and businesses had left, but President Reagan's trickle-down policies seemed to have worked, at least for Beale Street, and businesses and tourists were coming back. One of these newer places was the Rum Boogie, and right away, upon entering inside, it reminded me of The Bitter End in Greenwich Village, but with more southern flair.

THE BUS

We inquired at the bar for the manager and were told he'd come around later. We ordered drinks and took seats towards the side of the stage. The band was hitting the blues classics hard, Memphis style. Songs like Hoochie Coochie Man, The Thrill is Gone, Little Red Rooster, and Manish Boy, pretty standard fare for a club date blues act. They were playing pretty loud, so I decided to pull out one of my harps and play along, but only at a level I could hear. The bass player, who was also the lead singer, noticed what I was doing. When the song ended, he pointed to me and said on the mic, "Can you really play that thang?" Embarrassed, I shook my head no and felt a little guilty that I may have crossed a line, but Rick and Shane blurted out, "Oh yeah, he can!" Fuckers. "Well, get his ass up here," he said, "and let's see what he can do."

The audience applauded. The bass player knew how to read the room, and this audience wanted to be entertained and he was going to give it to them. Shane and Rick were ready to drag me up there, but I decided I'd spare them the pleasure and reluctantly made my way to the stage. Once up there, the Bass player introduced himself as Big T. "What key?" he asked. "E," I replied. Big T leaned back towards the band and said, "Mojo, in E." Another classic and a big hit for Muddy Waters. 'Got My Mojo Working' was a cryptic tale of a heartbroken man's failure to use Voodoo to attract his beloved. "I got my Mojo working, but it just won't work on you." Some people would say it's a metaphor for a musician not getting the audience excited. Believe me, that was foremost on my mind. But I knew the tune well and added accents and underscore around Big T's vocals. The band was really good, and they definitely made me play and sound much better.

When it came time for a solo, Big T nodded towards me, and I jumped into the fire. After my first 12 bars soloing, I moved over by the guitar player and looked right at him. When I got his attention, I started mimicking what he was doing. He picked up on it and tried to shake me. Now we were dueling. The audience loved it. At the end of the next 12 bars, I moved back to my original position and got out of the way for Big T to come back in with the vocals and the ending. He loved it. "What else you got?" he asked. And we did this for the rest of the set. Afterward, Big T said to me, "I like your style, kid. How 'bout you come back tomorrow night, and we'll make it official. Fifty bucks plus tips, food, and drinks." I was stunned. Of course, I wanted to do it. But would the guys want me to? He noticed my hesitation. "Hey, no obligation. You show up, you play." I couldn't argue that, so we made a deal. The manager we were hoping to meet came and went while I was onstage, so technically, we had to come back the next night and try again anyway. Returning back to the bus, Anthony and Mitch told us they got caught by one of the parking attendants hanging out in the bus and he warned us that the lot wasn't a hotel and that we couldn't sleep there. We decided to have a band meeting. We all agreed to chip in for a cheap motel room so we could use a shower and make some phone calls. We also agreed to stay in Memphis another night to try and catch the manager of the Rum Boogie. But it was too late to do all this in the moment so we had to pretend that we were leaving the bus and attempt to sneak back in later. We grabbed a bottle of JD and some smokes and decided to walk back to the river. It was a warm, beautiful, full-moon night.

The next day, we pulled the bus out of the lot, picked up bread, cold cuts, and beer at the grocery store, and moved to a budget hotel not too far from where we were. We got a single room and each took turns using the shower. We ate sandwiches, drank beer, and strummed guitars. Some folks staying at the hotel came by to check out the bus and see who we were. We shared our beer and smoked joints with them. They had never been to New York before and heard that it was dirty and full of criminals. There were other folks who were obviously avoiding us and seemed perturbed by our big blue bus and all the partying in the parking lot. One thing was for sure: it felt good to be clean. Now, we had to decide what our next move was. I followed up on a bunch of phone calls for gigs, and one of them actually came through. A place called the Backroom in Austin Texas. It would be about a ten-hour drive, probably longer because of the bus's fifty-mile-per-hour limit. It would have been nice if some other gigs would have come through that were along the way but we were happy we had something.

The Backroom. Probably a tiny hole in the wall in nowhere Texas we thought. We would see how the meeting would go at the Rum Boogie and take it from there. That night, I unpacked some stage clothes to wear for the show with Big T and his Cadillac Band, as they were known. I had a black and white embroidered shirt, a silver mohair suit jacket, a steer skull bolo, a wide denim Fedora hat with a leather band around it, and a pair of Cuban-heeled Chelsea boots in flat black. I pulled my long, curly hair into a ponytail and sealed the deal with a pair of mirrored aviator shades. I filled every pocket with a different key harp. We picked up some flasks during the day and filled them with whiskey. This way, we could order one drink from the bar and top it off with our own supply. Alcoholic Economics 101.

I brought a press kit with me to leave at the bar just in case we missed the manager again. The boys were doing bumps and trading pills. For me, coke and playing Harp do not mix. It shortens the breath and numbs the face. Weed, on the other hand, is just the right buzz for playing Blues. The Blues isn't about playing every note on the page perfectly. It's about following a feeling and praying for magic to happen. It's something indescribable, beyond words. Once we were feeling pretty good, we headed out to the club. When we got there, Big T was at the Bar, and I walked over to him, and we shook hands. He had an amazing poker face, but I could tell he was happy to see me. He said, "I see you brought your game."

I'm pretty sure he was referring to my attire. I chatted with the bartender and left the press kit with her for safekeeping. There weren't that many people in the audience yet, but I didn't care. I was excited to play real blues with real players. Playing the Harp was so freeing after being a drummer for so many years and having to shlep an entire drum kit around. Even with The Dirty Rain, I had to sing and be the front man, which has its own baggage because engaging with the audience is my responsibility. But tonight, I can just play. After getting our drinks, Big T pointed to me and then to the stage. Show time. And play we did. It all clicked. It was spontaneous, improvisational, chemistry right from the start, no warm-up, and it was fun. More people started to come into the club. Some people got up to dance. The music changed everything. The band seemed happy, but I really think they were just getting a kick out of seeing me, this skinny punk, totally in bliss. I was so young and green but open enough to connect with their seasoned musicianship; something fresh came out of something marinated. That's the magic flavor I was talking about, and it transformed me. I heard differently, saw differently, time somehow seemed less relevant, less fleeting, like from now on, I could just be.

We played a couple of sets, and the good vibes continued at the bar after the show. We were energized. Everyone was smoking, drinking, telling stories. The Blues seemed so far away in New York, but here in Memphis, it was in the air, in the voices, and in the whiskey. And we soaked it all in. It was also the beginning of a not-so-healthy habit of forgoing eating food for alcohol. At least, that was the case for me. I didn't like to eat before going on stage. Especially if I'm singing or playing Harp, I can't connect with my diaphragm if my stomach is heavy and I don't feel light. Alcohol, on the other hand, was not a problem; in fact, it worked wonders on my nerves and self-esteem, but it seemed I had begun to build up a resistance to it, to the point where I needed to drink a lot to feel its effects. Like Tom Waits said, "There's a lifestyle that's there before you arrive, and you're introduced to it."

And then you become best friends. So, between binge drinking hard liquor and not eating, I was practically hallucinating. I totally forgot to track down the manager to talk business, and if I didn't do it, it didn't get done. Besides, I was so grateful for the gig that I spent the money Big T gave me buying the musicians in the band drinks. The bartender blurted out, "Last Call!". We all stepped out and kept the party going right outside the front door of the bar.

I'm pretty sure the blow candy was flowing because everyone was speaking at the same time and way over-emphasizing words and gestures. Or maybe I was still hallucinating. There were a few satellites of the opposite sex orbiting around our high-flying party. A couple of the guys from The Cadillac Band wanted to check out our bus so the whole lot of us headed towards the hotel. One of the girls on the peripheral moved quickly, catching me from falling on my face from tripping over my own feet. She took my hand and slipped her arm around my waist. She practically carried me all the way. It was sweet. People loved hanging out on the bus. I guess it was like finding a hidden speakeasy or an out-of-the-way hipster bar. We always had plenty of Sharpies around for people to tag, draw, or write messages on the interior of the bus. Perhaps because it was a school bus, it was like we were kids getting away with something we shouldn't be doing. We were breaking all the bus rules, smoking, drinking, graffitiing, and eventually, sex. In the morning, I woke up on the shitty mattress in the back of the bus, terribly hungover, possibly still drunk, and very sticky.

The girl was long gone, but I could feel her all over me. There was a lot of stomping and clanking going on in the front of the bus. Annoyed, I struggled, lifting my head and peering over the amplifiers to see what the disturbance was. "It's Alive," chuckled Mitch mockingly. "Hell, can't we keep it down for a few more hours?" I pleaded. They were packing. "Time to clean up, rock star. The Honeymoon is over, and we gotta go." Instructed Shane. "Time is up on the room, and it's only a matter of minutes till we are kicked out of here," he added. "Go, go where?" I croaked. "The great state of Texas." He replied. "Dallas, Houston, Austin, and San Antonio, take your pick." Turns out, while I was supposedly hitting home runs in the back of the bus, Big T mentioned to the boys that we should head to Texas because the music scene was much bigger and more open-minded. Memphis was good for classic blues and rockabilly but less forgiving for the heavy sounds we were doing. Besides, we already had a confirmed gig. It made sense, but I was still disappointed. I begged the cleaning lady to do our room last and got to have a long, soapy shower and shave. I could feel my body saying, "What the hell are you doing to yourself?" I needed a drink. The boys were literally waiting for me with the bus running as I was getting my stuff out of the room. As soon as I stepped in, the door closed. Rick put it in gear, and Shane cranked up the stereo. They were torturing me.

We still had a few days before the gig in Austin, so Shane wanted to make a detour to Lubbock, Texas, the birthplace of Buddy Holly. I had no idea he was such a tourist. Buddy Holly never quite hit me the way Little Richard, Chuck Berry, and Bo Diddley did, although, 'Rave On' was very cool. And besides, everyone else was into it, and I was in no condition to argue. The point Shane was making wasn't lost on me. Here we were, on a bus and on a road trip that was starting to turn into a pilgrimage. When I think of Buddy, I think of all the artists who have based much of their careers on his style and others who have re-recorded his songs, like The

Ramones, Elvis Costello, The Clash, Blondie, and The Stones. All artists I could not live without. And how rock & roll's affiliation with danger only heightened after Buddy Holly, Richie Valens, and the Big Bopper all died in a plane crash, spreading further the legends and mysteries of rock mythology that I often wondered about when I was a kid.

I'm old enough to remember the deaths of Jimi Hendrix, Janis Joplin, and Jim Morrison still fresh my older sibling's minds. This was the peace sign, drug-induced, love generation, having their existential asses handed to them. I felt bad and embarrassed for them, but also, at the same time, extremely proud because they took a chance. They showed faith in creativity and braved the unknown, but I learned from that moment in time not to take anyone's word about anything. I began asking myself, was I following a tradition? Honestly and consciously, I would say no because, in my mind, I'm a renegade, following my own path, making my own choices, creating my own life. But subconsciously, maybe I am really just programmed by arch types. I believed in rock & roll. I believed rock & roll could change the world because I actually witnessed it with my own ears.

In 1967, The Monterey Pop Festival galvanized the counterculture with the "Summer of Love." James Brown unified a troubled audience at a Boston concert when Martin Luther King Jr. was fatally shot in 1968; the Concert for Bangladesh by George Harrison and Ravi Shankar in 1971 raised awareness and relief for refugees from East Pakistan. And in 1978 at the One Love Peace Concert in Jamaica, Bob Marley brought together rival gang members and leaders of the PNP and JLP. But congruent with all of these stories runs the dark side. Not long after Monterey, we lost Jimi Hendrix, Janis Joplin, Jim Morrison, and Brian Jones to drug abuse. James Brown was convicted on drug charges and assaulting a police officer and went to prison. George Harrison and his wife were brutally assaulted in their home, and Bob Marley and his family were ambushed and shot. Buddy Holly, Richie Valens, and the Big Bopper flew to their demise so as not to spend another frozen night in the tour bus with a broken heater. Is rock & roll a death wish? All these kids, since the 50s waiting for nuclear bombs to fall from the sky. At that point, you got to say 'fuck it' because today could be your last.

THE OUT OF TOWNERS

We had a good twelve-to-fifteen-hour drive to Lubbock unless we stopped in Dallas, which was along the way. It got so hot in the bus we would open up the two emergency exits on the top of the bus, and it wasn't long before we started to stick our heads out the top and then eventually our entire bodies, laying back on the roof and using our legs as anchors. It was a lot of fun and stupidly dangerous. Watching the stars at night was the most magical. We were also putting huge dents in those Jack Daniel's cases. I knew the worst thing I could do was to start drinking again, but that's exactly what I did. We were leaving the South East and entering the Midwest, and we wanted to celebrate. It was uncharted territory for all of us. Most people from New York have parents or grandparents from the Old World. American patriotism for New Yorkers is expressed by the freedom of representing your old-world heritage. The further one gets from New York, the more that expression changes to a national identity. The further we got from New York, the more we felt that difference. We weren't used to seeing so many American flags everywhere. Much of the United States in the early Eighties experienced an economic boom compared to the recession that plagued the Seventies. President Reagan's "It's Morning in America" galvanized at least half the country, and for some, American pride was to be celebrated.

Ironically, that would all come crashing down on Black Monday, but we weren't there yet. New York City in the Eighties was a whole other story. Out-of-control crime, drugs, homelessness, pollution, and AIDs sent overwhelmed urbanites running for the suburbs. The New York Stock Exchange and multinational corporate culture became synonymous with avarice and materialism. Instead of morning in America, for us, it was hungover in New York. We felt like we were in a different country. Outside the windows of both sides of the bus were acres of farmland as far as the eye could see. So much land, sky, and space can change one's perspective. Living in New York, nature and farmlands become abstract concepts you may occasionally encounter on a weekend trip upstate, and the thought of where the mountains of food products packed into supermarkets and served in restaurants came from is rarely acknowledged.

In fact, as rock and rollers, we prided ourselves on how much urban grease and squalor we could stand, utilizing it as a gauge of how authentically sleazy we were. The philosophy was if we were fearless, we would become one with the toxins, and hence they would have no effect on us. Ironically, now that we were far out from the cities, our internal toxicity was much more obvious. All the wide-open vistas were having an effect on our little gang of urban pirates. Between the windows, whiskey, and weed, we would veg out, staring at the fields rolling by. Were we contemplating, self-reflecting, or just stoned? Rick made an executive DJ decision and stopped the Bowie cassette that was playing and switched to the radio. Country music filled the bus for the first time. There was a collective chuckle. It was a good call. We had never listened to country music together before, and I believe Shane was the only one who had a slight interest in it. I remember when I was four or five years old, 'Boy Named Sue' by Johnny Cash was one of my first favorite songs but was quickly outshined by Grand Funk Railroad's 'Tell Everybody You Know, You Got That Rock & Roll Soul." But every once in a while, I would be in the mood for some Hank Williams, Waylon Jennings, or even Tammy Wynette. But my favorite country artist was also my favorite soul artist, Ray Charles. His album, Country Western Meets Rhythm and Blues, was a revelation to me as a kid that some artists are just way above genres and labels. Damn, one of my favorite albums of all time is Ray's 'The Spirit of Christmas. I could listen to that in the middle of summer. It's so funky, but out here in the middle of the United States of America, the sound that came out of the radio seemed to blend in with the views and the hum of the wheels and motor.

After driving all day with the sun in our eyes and nothing but green in our peripheral, the landscape began succumbing to street lights, fast food restaurants, and shopping centers. As we slowed down for an intersection, a pair of long-toned legs in high heels, a skin-tight mini skirt, and a pile of curly blond hair were sashaying down the sidewalk just ahead of us. Everyone's eyes popped out of their heads, just like an old Tex Avery cartoon. We wrestled each other towards the front of the bus. As Rick slowly crept our vehicle up behind the shapely Venus, Mitch opened the front door, leaned out, and crooned, "Excuse me, Miss, can you tell us which way to Dallas?" Without losing a beat, our temptress whips her head around, revealing a brutally crooked nose and a mouth full of missing teeth from which she spat out the words, "Where the fuck ya think yer at, pecker head!" Mitch nearly fell on his ass as Rick slammed down on the gas pedal, jerking the bus forward, and the rest of us busted up, laughing ourselves to tears. Welcome to Texas!

After regaining our composure, we needed to park the bus and find some food. One thing all of us agreed on was barbeque. I've had Carolina pulled pork, Tennessee pit-smoked, Alabama white sauce, and Kentucky dipped mutton, but this would be the first time having authentic Dallas, Texas barbeque.

We started asking people in cars with their windows down where the nearest real down-home barbeque could be found. More than a couple of times we heard Back Country Bar-B-Q mentioned and got all kinds of directions. Miraculously, we found the place. Luckily, it was right off the main highway and there was a huge parking lot perfect for the bus. Man, we must have looked like a freak show pulling into that place. No markings on a midnight blue tinted window school bus with New York plates. We parked as far away from the building as we could and piled out of the bus like sea-legged sailors. We were drunk, high, stoned, and hungry. The inside of the restaurant was huge and wide open. It smelled of smoked meat and sautéed greens. There were Mooseheads and flags on the walls. There were quite a few people at the counter, but not many sitting at the numerous tables. It turned out that they were near closing time. That was a bummer, but we decided to order anyway and eat on the bus. The prices were pretty reasonable. I believe we ordered every meat they had: beef, pork, chicken, turkey, and a ton of sides. This, for me, was one of the best excuses for traveling, finding, and eating the local cuisine. I do not know how to explain it, but I feel it is an accord between the visitors and the locals. The local says, 'Try our food, and then you will understand who we are and act accordingly.' For me, this builds character, and by obliging, the visitor shows courage and acceptance. For me, food, music, and stories are the ambassadors of the world. We were happy in our place, in the parking lot of a barbeque restaurant on the edges of Dallas, with our food and our bus. Life was good.

We ate and drank ourselves to sleep in that restaurant parking lot as we were very tired. The bus wasn't conducive to long-distance travel with the shaking and banging taking a toll on the senses, plus always being hungover surely didn't help. It was much easier to sleep when the bus wasn't moving, but our blissful dreams came crashing down with a harsh bang from the front door of the bus. As I slowly opened my eyes, I could see red and blue lights flashing outside, and for a second, I had no idea who or where I was. Then I heard everyone waking up. It was the cops. Shit! The one hard rule we had was not to keep drugs on our person and always, when we were diving, to stash them in our designated hiding spot, which was inside the interior of one of the original bus seats. I had no idea if anyone had decided to forgo that rule, and I suddenly realized this could be really bad. I went to the front of the bus and opened the door. A flashlight blinded me. I raised my hand to block the light, and a voice from the void said in a thick drawl, "Put yer fucking hand down." I did. "Licenses and registration." Barked the voice. Rick crawled towards me and handed me his wallet. I handed it to the blinding light and then opened the glove compartment for the registration. The flashlight turned to the documents now in the officers' hands. I could see through the window there were two cars outside so I knew there was at least one more cop out there. Pointing the light back in my face he says, "Everybody out of the bus." Fuck. This sucked. We all spilled out into the glare of flashing red and blue light. How poetic, I thought.

There were two other officers that I could see. Everybody played it cool since we've all had our time dealing with cops in multiple situations, and we all knew nothing we could do or say was going to make the situation any better. "Don't move." Said the cop with the flashlight as he proceeded to enter the bus. I could see his light darting back and forth as he surveyed the interior of the big blue whale. He seemed not to be touching anything, just shining the light. A few seconds more he comes off the bus. He walks right up to Rick, hands him back his wallet and the registration, and says, "What's the story here, Rick?" Without a flinch, Rick takes back the documents and says, "We're a band from New York, on our way to Los Angeles, stopped here for some food, and fell asleep." The cop took a few seconds to stare right into Rick's eyes. Rick stared right back. "Ok, friends," said the cop, "I want you to get back on that bus and make your way to Los Angeles. Is that understood?" We all looked at each other and said, "Yes, sir!" and, without hesitation, ran back into the bus and closed the door behind us. Rick took the driver's seat and started it up and gunned it out of there. We could see the highway from the restaurant and headed straight for it. Oh my God, did we just dodge a bullet? It seemed so. That was lucky. But what wasn't so lucky was when we started the bus, the oil light came on, and as we pulled out of our parking spot, keeping our eyes on the cops, we could see a big ole puddle of oil reflecting the flashing lights. Our pirate ship had sprung a leak.

The cops hadn't followed, which meant they didn't want to deal with us, and we didn't want to give them a reason to. But we were going to have to stop somewhere and check the oil. The question was when and where. The sun was just coming up, and we were still groggy. Nothing was open. We decided to pick somewhere where we could quickly check the oil and map where we were and where we were going. We let a few exits pass by to give us some distance from the police. Then we saw a gas station that sort of looked open. We took the exit and pulled in. It was closed, but it had all the lights on. Maybe they were about to open. We turned off the engine, got out, and quickly popped the hood to check the oil; it was way low, not even hitting the dipstick. As Shane replenished the oil, the rest of us checked the map. We all agreed we should drive some more just to get further from those cops and then find a service station and deal with the bus. But in which direction? Lubbock was out of the way, but we still had time before we had to be in Austin. We figured, what the hell, Lubbock it is. Somewhere on the edge of Fort Worth, we stopped at a service station.

Luckily, they were nice enough to take a quick look to see if they could even help us. Turns out it was just a worn gasket and they had the replacement part in stock. We asked if they could also take a look at the brake lines. We kept having to slightly pump the brakes more and more since we had left New York. They said no problem. Now, it was just a matter of time. Anthony and Mitch headed out on foot to get some food. The gasket installation took about an hour and cost $175. It was the first time I used a credit card. The brakes were a different story, and that would cost a lot more and take a lot more time. We decided to continue on our way for now since it hadn't become that big of a problem yet. We were defiantly feeling sobered after our brush with the Dallas police in the morning and the issues with the bus. Hopefully, Lubbock would be worth it. Back on the highway, the landscape changed again, getting dryer, hotter and dustier. We could see for miles in every direction, and the sun was bright. We were entering the West, and it made me feel as if I was at the bottom of a dried-up ocean.

As we pulled into Lubbock, there we literally tumble weeds rolling down the streets like a cartoon. Not many cars were on the road, and we didn't see many people walking around. The Buddy Holly statue was listed on our map, so we drove right to it. Today, the statue is no longer in the same place it was when we visited it in the 80s. They have since moved it and have added a memorial and a museum, and probably have way more tourism happening, but for us, we nearly missed it as we drove by. We swung the bus around to take another look. Yup, that was it. A statue of Buddy Holly and not much of anything else around, just an occasional car passing by. There were no places to park the big blue whale near the statue so we drove down some side streets and pulled over.

Some of us would go check it out first, and some would stay with the bus, and then we would switch. We were still paranoid from our morning brush with the law. Myself, Rick, and Shane went first since we were more historically interested so to speak. The air was dusty, and the sun was strong. We strolled towards the statue. Another dead rock and roller. Between the surroundings, the climate, and the statue, I suddenly became depressed and a little lonely. We brought our flasks with us and raised a toast to Buddy. Damn, I hoped Austin would be better. We decided not to hang in Lubbock but instead try to make it to Austin by early evening, and by taking turns driving, that wouldn't be a problem. We figured we'd stop along the way for food and gas. We were eager to keep moving. At this time, the city of Austin hadn't solidified its place on the rock and roll map with the South-by-South-West festival, better known as SXSW. We didn't know then that it would become one of the most important music festivals in the world, but Austin had always been known as a music town, and the meteoric rise of Stevie Ray Vaughn definitely put the spotlight on the city.

After being on the road for a few hours, we decided to pull over at a roadside restaurant that had a sign out front advertising Chicken Fried Steak and Gravy. What the hell was a Chicken Fried Steak? With a name like that, I definitely wanted to find out. The place was smokey and filled with plump, burly truck drivers; even the waitresses were stretching the seams of their uniforms. Comparatively, we looked like wet, emaciated alley cats, but it felt good to all sit together at a proper table and order some food. I ordered the Chicken Fried Steak, mashed potatoes, biscuits, gravy, and a beer. When it arrived, it was a giant piece of meat, battered and fried, on a huge plate, covered in a white gravy sauce. With my first tasting, I recognized the taste as a German Schnitzel with a kind of milky Hollandaise sauce. I liked it. As we ate, we discussed the possibility of getting a rehearsal room when we got to town, just so we could run through the set list and make sure all the gear was working. The steak was great, but if I was eating that all the time, I'd be round and burly too. Feeling quite satiated, we didn't waste time and got right back on the road. We ended up pulling into Austin later than we thought. We had no idea where to go other than the venue. I imagined in my mind The Back Room as a tiny dive bar, probably not even a stage, and with just a small vocal p.a. Lord knows I had played enough of those kinds of places. You know, the neighborhood bar, where locals meet every weekend to watch local bands try out their amateur songs or popular covers, and maybe once in a while, a band like us breezes through town to be the zoo animals for a night.

As we came down the road, we saw this huge marquee sign with block letters spelling out 'The Back Room.' We had arrived, and it was nothing like we had expected. It was a large shaped, stand-alone building. Were we in the right place? We pulled into the parking lot where there were lots of action, cars, and people, or more accurately, pick-up trucks and Cowboys and Cowgirls. We saw a Winnebago parked in the lot and pulled up on the opposite side of it to kind of hide the bus. Still paranoid about the cops, Rick and Anthony hung back to do a maintenance check while Shane, Mitch, and I headed into the club. There was a cover charge to get in, but we told the door person we were playing the next night and just drove from New York, and since we've never been there before, could we please just check the place out? They politely obliged. Inside was massive with several sections, an area with tables and chairs, a huge pool room, and a proper concert stage with a lighting rig and a full range p.a. system and on-stage monitors. We were blown away. It would be the biggest stage we've played as a band so far. There was an engineer at the front-of-house soundboard that we introduced ourselves to. We learned from him that we were playing with three other bands on a night specifically for unsigned bands. There was no cover charge and no flat rates.

All four bands would split a percentage of the bar's take. Under those circumstances, we didn't expect to see much more than pocket change, but at least the venue was solid, and we'd be able to do a sound check, which was a rarity in New York clubs. I suddenly felt intimidated. Even though we've played some big stages like The Middle East in Boston or Lamour's in New York, at those places, I felt like I was on the home team's field.

We were definitely not on home turf here. One of the staff showed us where we would load in and where the dressing rooms were. We asked her if it was safe to park and stay on the bus overnight. She recommended a truck stop just out of town and warned about cops coming down hard on parking illegally in the city but that the bus was safe for now if we wanted to get Anthony and Rick to join us. We headed back to the bus to get the boys and fill the flasks. With all of us inside together, we headed straight for the pool tables. When it came to playing pool, we were all pretty much compatible, which made it interesting, and we usually played for money or drinks. One of us would have to wait his turn, so I volunteered and went to get the drinks.

Playing on a table near to us were two very cute hippie girls, playing pool but not taking it seriously, missing shots, balls flying off the table, falling down laughing, and really putting on a show. They were probably tipsy or just acting like it. I hit the bar and ordered whiskeys all around. One of the cute hippie girls appeared at the bar next to me and ordered two beers. We made eye contact, and both of us smiled. "Hey!" I said, "Would you mind helping me bring these drinks over to my friends at the table next to yours?" She smiled back. "Sure!" she said in a curly Texas drawl. "Your beers are on me," I said and paid the bartender. "That is awfully sweet of you, darlin'," she replied and we both headed back to the pool tables and made our introductions. "I'm Holly." "I'm Lizzy," they said. After some small talk, the boys continued their game, which was getting serious, so I played with the girls. They were having fun teasing me by slapping each other's butts as they took turns taking shots and kissing each other when they sank a ball. After a while, a few of their friends showed up and invited us outside to smoke a joint. We, in turn, invited them to hang out on the bus. I loved seeing the faces of people when they first entered the bus. It was like they were entering a spaceship or time machine. Turns out the hippy girls loved to draw, and right away, they grabbed the markers and got to work.

While many joints were passed around, the bus became a centrifugal force for folks coming out of the club until we had a full-on party on our hands that kept rocking till the club closed. As the employees made their way to their cars, they recommended that we not stay in the lot all night. We got the hint. The girls offered to lead us with their car to the overnight truck stop on the outskirts of town, and all of a sudden, I felt like we were living in a ZZ Top song. We drove for about twenty minutes on the state highway till we came to an off-ramp that led to a large parking lot filled with several semi-18 wheelers and a gas station and diner. We parked as far away from the trucks and buildings as we could.

The girls parked, came on the bus just to say goodnight and said that they would see us at the show and try to get people to come. They were sweethearts. After they left, we stayed up a while longer smoking cigarettes, drinking beer, listening to music, and discussing our now nightly routine of who's sleeping where. We were excited about the show and the venue, so the mood was good. We fell asleep to the sounds of the Trucks idling in the lot.

We were passed out almost till noon, and it was rough getting ourselves together because it was already broiling hot on the bus. We were all dehydrated, low on water and basic supplies, and desperately needed to be hosed down. We stunk. Noticing the night before that one of the buildings we passed while entering was a diner, we decided to start our day there. We walked toward the place looking greasy and ragged, all of us in sunglasses, carrying our personal compact oral hygiene packs. At the walkway leading to the entrance was a life-size cut-out sign of a cartoon potbellied cowboy with blue jeans, a flannel shirt, boots, and a ten-gallon hat that practically covered its entire face except for the mouth, his right hand lifted up at the elbow and a big thumb sticking straight up, with a word bubble attached to it, and a command written in bold bubble letters saying, "COME ON IN!" We stopped, looked, and chuckled. The place was busy, filled with truckers, migrants, and family travelers and we definitely got some 'surprised' looks as we entered. A highly caffeinated, plump waitress in a brown uniform and pink apron seated us and offered coffee and water, which we did not refuse. Thankfully, they did breakfast all day, so we filled up on bacon and eggs. We ended up having a conversation with the waitress.

She said everyone was curious about who we were. They didn't get many New York City rock and roll-looking dudes pulling in on a painted blue school bus. We asked where was a good supermarket nearby but she said it was best to shop back in town. We all took turns using the bathroom to clean up as much as we could. When we were done, we had one more cup of coffee and made our plan of attack. We never did get a rehearsal to warm up before the gig. We trusted the venue was well-equipped and that we'd be ok. We discussed a basic setlist. We had 10 original songs, some old-school rockers like Wild Thing, Train Kept a Rolling, some funk by Sly and the Family Stone and James Brown, and then random blues jams in different keys and grooves. We only had an hour on stage, so we decided to do all the original songs. We figured, what the heck, let's see if they worked.

Back at the bus, we lifted the mattress off the gear and took out the guitars and drums and gave them a quick status check. Other than the drum heads needing some tightening, everything seemed fine. We reorganized the packing so everything we needed for the gig was easily accessible. The vibe was a little tense. I was definitely feeling nervous and anxious. I guess we were all feeling a bout of imposter syndrome coming on, especially me. Singing and fronting a band was still a new experience, and up to this point, I had done way more gigs from behind the drums than in front of them. Some of my biggest influences came from Texas, like Lightning Hopkins, Janis Joplin, Stevie Ray Vaughn, and Edgar and Johnny Winter, for starters. One thing all these artists have in common is a high level of musicianship, especially with guitars. In our band's aesthetic, there was quite a bit of punk and glam, which basically means it's more of an attitude and a primitive sound that gets expressed, sometimes at the expense of musical skill, but still an art form in itself. In many ways, it's a New York thing, going back to bands like The New York Dolls, Television, and The Ramones. Because in New York, sound systems were usually blown out, mixing board operators were usually hearing impaired, and the audiences were usually coked to the gills, bands relied on volume, energy, and visuals to get the feeling across, and we were no exception. We hoped that our Texas friends would relate or, at best, appreciate our enthusiasm and our limitations.

Feeling like we had the packing together, we got on the bus and headed to town for supplies, which mostly meant beer, cigarettes, and gas. Austin in the

1980s wasn't as internationally famous for music as it is now, but regionally it was known to have some of the best music in the country. There was definitely more of a local, almost family vibe back then than there is now. Downtown had Austin City Limits, custom cowboy hat and boot stores, barbeque restaurants, and the most long-haired dudes we've seen since leaving New York. There was a youthful energy in the air, without the burden of a long history like Nashville or Memphis to live up to. After wasting too much time parking and shopping, we were off to the club for load-in and sound check.

KICK OUT THE JAMS

There's always a grounding feeling I get when setting up the band gear on an unfamiliar stage in an unfamiliar town as if it creates a familiar home within a strange place. A four-piece drum kit, a guitar amp, and a bass amp were what we were: simple and raw. Since we were the last band of the night, we were the first to sound-check. Our gear went right from the bus to the stage. The Back Room's stage managers were professional and personable. We all had individual monitors with independent mixes. When the microphones and direct lines were in place, we did a quick line check, which meant the sound board operator made sure all the sound sources were going to the correct channels before we actually all played together. Once he was satisfied, we kicked into one of our originals.

After a few measures we stopped and expressed to the engineer what we individually needed to hear in our monitors. We did this several times till we all felt comfortable. For a low-level band, this was a real treat.

Usually, there was only one monitor mix, if there were even any monitors at all. It makes a difference how a band feels and how a band plays. Our half-hour was up, so we had to make way for the next band. There were three other bands besides ourselves and we decided to hang around for their sound checks and check out the competition. We learned that none of them were local. All three other bands were also going from town to town, gig to gig, but they all had a much more distinct 80s dance-pop sound compared to our hard rock roots vibe. Another perk of this gig was that each band had its own dressing room, with mirrors, hangers, and beers in a cooler. For most of our shows, all the bands share just one dressing room, which can be both a lot of fun or a disaster, depending on the situation. After the sound checks, each band retreated into their respective dressing rooms. We dug into the cooler and started drinking the beers, and of course, we snuck in our flasks.

After a while, the crowd started to trickle in. There were a lot of cowboy hats and boots and beer bellies filling up the place. It seemed to be a more rural crowd than the night before, and even the pre-show music had more country rock songs mixed in. I had that nervous feeling again. The first band took the stage, and they were good, but nobody was paying attention to them. People were playing pool or at the bar, but no one came up to the stage or applauded between songs. They finished their set, and it was anti-climactic. The second band had it even worse. In between songs you could hear shouts from the back of the club saying, 'Go Home!' or 'You Suck!' It was not a good vibe. By the third band, the crowd was getting rowdy and drunk and some of them were now approaching the stage. A couple of good ole boys started to shake their beer bottles and released the spray towards the stage, followed by a few limes and ice cubes. Now we were freaking out.

The heckling was getting progressively worse, and we were on next. Inside our dressing room, I sat the boys down to come up with a plan. I suggested we change gears and open with Sly and the Family Stone's 'I Want to Take You Higher.' It was always a crowd pleaser, and the lyrics were a direct communication with the audience to raise the vibration! I don't know why, but something just told me it would work. The third band ended their set early, which gave us a little extra time to get set up. As I walked onto the stage, I was so nervous my knees started knocking together uncontrollably. I had never experienced that before. It was obvious we looked nothing like this audience and now they've gathered around the stage to continue their torturous fun. I could see the cute hippy girls were out there and they had a decent size crew with them. At least we would have some people on our side. When we were ready, like Bob Dylan said to The Band during the 1966 Manchester England show, I shouted, "Play it fucking loud"! I blasted my Harmonica into the microphone for the opening Sly riff, and we were off. Right away, the crowd took a step back. We shouted into the mics, "Hey, Hey, Hey, Hey," like the song goes and that infectious groove pushed hard through the P.A. Then I noticed the heads of the audience starting to bop up and down, and then their asses started to shake, and I knew then we had them.

THE BUS

I knew we were having a great show with the rare sight of the boys smiling on stage, which wasn't typical. And even the members of the other bands joined in dancing with the audience. I was so relieved, I actually relaxed, and with the monitors tuned, it sounded like I could actually sing. We played for over an hour, and when we finished, we got an encore. ZZ Top's 'Tush' was the perfect call. We walked off the stage, exhausted and covered in sweat. Right away, these rancher-looking dudes, and what I guessed were their wives, came up to us and said they would buy us some shots, and of course, we obliged. At the bar, the bartender filled rows of tumblers with whiskey, and those good old boys passed them around. Anthony held up the tumbler they handed him and said, "I thought you all said we were gonna do a shot?" They responded with, "Round here, that is a shot," "More like three shots," I said, and with a wink, and down the hatch that golden brown nectar of the gods flowed. The good ole boys wanted to drink us under the table, but they didn't realize we'd been drinking for days. After a few more rounds, each one of them eventually ended up heaving their guts out in the bathroom. In all fairness, we definitely had the advantage of being on a bender already, but by the look on their wives' faces, we figured it was time to mosey.

They paid us $100 bucks, and then we followed the hippy girls and their crew outside to party on the bus. Outside in the parking lot, the Back Room turned into a tailgate party. The lot was filled with long hair, cowboy hats, miniskirts, mohawks, pickup trucks, Camaros, and Harleys; even some low riders and hip-hop cruisers were pulling in. It was getting out of hand, to say the least. Again, the bus was the centrifugal force. I held the court as the boys packed the gear. Everyone was drinking, smoking, revving engines, breaking bottles, blasting music, and shooting fireworks. These two well-dressed dudes who caught our show asked how long we were in town. I told them it was loose but that we were on our way to Los Angeles for a gig at The Whisky, and they mentioned that they worked for a promotion company connected to The Austin Chamber of

Commerce and asked could we stop by their office later in the week to discuss booking some shows? I took their card and told them we would be in touch, and they left to join the party. The parking lot was raging, but eventually, the cops showed up, and the exodus began. The hippy girls swung by and said to meet them at the truck stop that we had stayed at the night before, and then they got in their cars. Even as Rick started the bus, people were still on board, so we just closed the doors and took off with them inside, we didn't want to get left behind with the law.

Thank God the cops didn't follow us because everybody else did. We were like a rock and roll convoy, infesting the highway like locusts, raising a plume of dust in our wake. It was crazy when we pulled into that truck stop parking lot like warrior Indians circling the stagecoach in the old western movies. Following our modus operandi, we parked as far away from the building as possible. Everyone else pulled up next to us and spilled out of their vehicles into the lot. We turned up the music and opened the doors and the party resumed. Out of nowhere, this gorgeous girl appeared on the bus. She had very long, thick black hair, alabaster skin, and bright silver-blue eyes. She was wearing a baby blue short tapered skirt with white thigh-high silk stockings revealing her long elegant legs and a tight blue and white collared shirt unbuttoned way down, exposing a gold lace bra. She was writing something on the wall of the bus, having one knee on the couch and her other leg stretched behind her as she leaned over the top of the couch to access the exact spot she wanted. I moved towards her to see what she was writing. In almost perfect calligraphy were the words 'Private Joy Was Here.' "That's very mysterious," I said, trying to sound reasonably sober. She turned herself around, sat on the couch, and said, "Is this your bus?" She didn't have a Texas accent. Actually, she didn't have any accent at all. "As a matter of fact, it is," I replied. "And you drive around the country in it?" she inquired. "Yes," I said, "We're on our way to California from New York." "New York?" she flirtatiously repeated. Just then, I heard a shout from a female voice outside the bus, "Joy, are you in there?" The gorgeous girl answered back, "Yes!" "Ah," I said, "your name is Joy."

She reached out to me with the palm of her hand turned down. She was wearing black nail polish. I took her hand, lifted it to my lips, and kissed it as I introduced myself. Joy's friend entered the bus with a big smile and wide-open eyes scanning the interior. "Wow," she said, "this is very cool." "This is Casey," said Joy. "Hello, Casey," I said. "Welcome to our home." Joy handed Casey the marker she was using and gestured toward the wall. Casey understood and searched for her spot to tag. I kept thinking about what Joy had written, and then it came to me. "Private Joy," I said out loud. "Like the Prince song?" A look came over her face that had the effect of warming my entire body. "Very good?" she purred. "I love Prince!" she said almost growling. Then I understood her whole sexy style. That Eighties, Nu Romantic, Gothic Wave, Prince look with a touch of sex shop accessories. I was infatuated. "Can I offer you anything?" I asked. "Like what?" she replied. "Name your poison." I challenged. "I don't drink or do drugs." She shot back. "How 'bout I change the music to Prince?" I offered. She smiled and said, "I'll accept that." The album I chose to put on was 'Sign of the Times,' I had that double album on repeat since it came out, and to this day, it's still a masterpiece. In fact, I would say pop music today is just catching up to what Prince was already doing in the Eighties.

Extremely sparse recordings, almost demo-like, heavy on drum machine funk and ice-cold synth lines, and vocals way upfront in the mix, a combination of histrionic gospel-like falsettos and raw, husky, erotic rap. As the beginning groves of the title track bubbled out of the speakers, I went back and sat next to Joy. We lost track of time, sharing our Prince concert stories. By this time, everyone else was pairing off into their own worlds when the double album ended, and we could hear sounds of pleasure coming from the back of the bus. Joy and I quietly laughed at the awkward moment and I got up and changed the music to another very sexy double album, Princes' 1999. When I turned around, I saw

Joy had fully unbuttoned her top and was curling her black nail-polished finger, gesturing me to come to her, and I did not hesitate. I sat back down on the couch, and then she whipped her leg over and around me and sat on my lap, her beautiful soft flesh filling her gold lace bra, hovering in front of my face, her body dancing into mine in time with the music. The groove, the bus, and the bodies all became one, and then, at one point, everything disappeared, and all that was left was bliss.

When the sun came up, reality began to rear its ugly head. Like coming out of a coma, I could hear the tractor-trailers in the parking lot starting their engines and releasing their air brakes. Joy and I were holding each other as if it was the last time, and then there was Casey's voice again from outside the bus, but this time, in a half whisper, she called out, "Joy, we have to go." "Okay, give me a moment," Joy whispered back, jumped up, and swiftly put her clothes on. She paused, looked at me intensely, kissed me, and then, just as mysteriously as she arrived, she was gone. I watched them drive away into the rising sun through the dusty bus window like she was an angel from the southwest desert.

One after the other, the boys emerged from several cars in the lot, saying goodbye to their own private joys. The two hippy girls saw me looking through the window and waved. I think they were together. Slowly all the cars, trucks, and bikes rode away, and then there was just the bus and the wreckage left of bottles, cans, butts, and broken glass littering the parking lot. The boys crawled back onto the bus, and without a word, we simultaneously passed out. After what must have been a couple of hours, we were all abruptly woken up by violent banging on the bus door. Half asleep and half in shock, I thought, Damn the cops again? We and the bus were a smelly mess, and empty bottles and cans were everywhere. The banging was relentless. We all huddled together to face the truth. I took a deep breath, put my hand on the door handle, and swung it open. We were all shocked to see this stout, rotund man, a parody of that cartoon cowboy cut-out character that was at the entrance of the diner, that had come to life; he even had his big ole thumb in the air, but instead of saying, come on in, in a thick Texas drawl he growled: "Get the fuck out!"

Damn, we were back on the road again and in no condition to be. We figured we needed another motel to wash and sober up, but we had no idea where to go. The sun was vicious bright, and the heat stifling. Getting a place close to town would be too expensive, so we decided to go the opposite way. Luckily, after driving for only about 20 minutes, we found a place. There weren't many cars in the lot and the sign out front said vacancy, so we pulled the big blue beast right on in. I went inside the office to book us a room while the boys attempted to tidy up the bus. After more than a few dirty looks from the motel desk clerk, I got us one double room so that we could take turns again washing the filth off our hides. Unfortunately, the only double rooms were on the second floor, so we had to carry the bags and guitars up the stairs. I was exhausted and fell face down on the bed and passed out, and by the time I got into the bathroom, it was totally trashed. We weren't the most considerate bunch but I was grateful anyway to finally get clean.

While changing my clothes, I found the business card those promoter dudes gave me the night before in my pocket, and after getting dressed, I used the phone in the room to call them. Dave picked up the phone and he seemed happy that I called. He stated that it was his mission to make Austin the live music capital of the world and wanted to feature national and international bands at local venues and that we would be a perfect fit. He also mentioned that he was interested in managing and producing bands and would we be interested in that? I told him definitely and that we had no other commitments other than our gig at The Whisky. He wanted to draft up a contract before we left and asked if we could hang around for a couple more days. I answered yes, but the soonest would be best. I figured it was probably best not to tell him about being kicked out of several lots already. We both agreed to check back in the next day and I thanked him for his time.

During the call, something was distracting the boys outside so after I hung up with Dave, I stepped out of the room and leaned over the second-floor railing, and as I imagined, the boys were entertaining some hotel guests by the bus. Of course, I joined in. Cars started pulling into the lot that weren't even looking for a motel but only because they recognized the bus. Out of one of the cars escaped a harem of girls, a couple of them who saw our show the night before but didn't hang for the tailgate party, all eagerly piling onto the bus, and as usual, we opened a celebratory bottle of Jack for the occasion. As the sun fell, our spirits rose, and some of us moved the party up to the hotel room.

I'm not sure exactly when or how it happened, but after what seemed like a long time of people just hanging around, watching TV on the beds and on the floor, all of a sudden, clothing started coming off simultaneously and, on an impulse, I started kissing the girl I was just having a casual conversation with. I didn't even remember her name from when she introduced herself on the bus earlier.

She slipped her eager hands under my clean t-shirt, and I responded by taking it off. Then she did the same with hers, and like long-separated lovers, we had our hands all over each other's bodies. I went for the top button of her jeans, but she took over and gracefully slipped them off. While all this was happening, I could see in my peripheral vision the same thing happening all around me, and then like a bolt of lightning, a rush of hot electricity filled my body, and I thought, Holy shit, I'm in an orgy, inside a Texas roadside motel room! And from that moment on, the night would become a blur of bodies without faces and voices without words. Although the experience was exhilarating, I could also feel a part of myself, my younger self, disappearing, and there was no turning back.

I don't remember when I fell asleep, but upon waking up the next morning, I realized what it must be like waking up after being knocked out from an explosion. My ears were ringing; there was crust in my eyes, and every muscle and bone in my body was throbbing. The bed was covered with several people in and on it who were out cold and snoring. The second bed was also filled with bodies and even a few more on the floor.

The TV was on as the sun started to peek through the curtains. I slowly crawled out of the bed, trying desperately not to disturb anyone and luckily found my pants under the bed and my shirt on top of the air conditioner. I found only one sock and boot, so I just stayed barefoot. I slipped out the door to get some fresh air and check on the bus. It was nice and cool, and the birds were chirping away. The concrete was cold on the soles of my feet, and it kind of sobered me up. I walked carefully to the bus and pushed the door slowly open. I walked the three steps up into the cabin that, unsurprisingly, also looked like where a bomb went off with bodies everywhere. I saw Shane's head raise up from under a pile of bodies on the couch. He pushed himself out naked, like a newborn baby out of a womb, and stretched his body as much as he could, letting out a roar. RAAAAHHHRRrrrrrr!!!! It was like he released something he'd been holding back for a long time, and then he looked at me with the softest smile I had ever seen on his face. Needless to say, he woke up the whole bus. I grabbed some cigarettes and a lighter and stepped outside. Shane clumsily followed me, totally buck naked and grabbing a beer. He didn't give a fuck. As I was smoking, people were walking down the stairs from the room like zombies. Eventually, the bus emptied out too. Nobody said a word, and if there was any eye contact, it was reciprocated with barely a nod, expressing a combination of gratitude, secrecy, and shame.

We were very lucky there weren't many people staying at the hotel at the time, and the ones that were there actually partied with us, but when I went back to the office to book the room another night, the clerk sternly asked us to please leave and that we wouldn't want to get the law involved. In complete agreement and understanding, I walked back to the room and told the boys the time had come and to get back on the bus. They knew we had taken it too far and were getting off easy, so no one complained. I called Dave while we still had the phone in the room and set up a meeting downtown. We cleaned ourselves and the room the best we could and then said goodbye to the few stragglers that were hanging around. Getting back onto the bus, we were all silent. It seemed like each of us were in our own heads. Rick took the driver's seat and started her up. We all huddled at the front of the bus, staring out into space thru the front window; then, at the perfect moment, a loud percussive fart broke the silence and the ice, and we all collapsed in swoons of laughter.

Dave's office was between a cowboy bootmaker and a restaurant that was more like a cafeteria. The parking spaces in front were not suitable for the bus, so we drove around the back and parked there. We split up to have someone watching the bus. Dave's office was a cubicle in a room with several other cubicles. We shook hands and told him we had parked the bus out back. I could see in his eyes he'd forgotten about the bus, but after a slight hesitation, he suggested we go where all of us could join the meeting and also keep our eyes on the bus. We followed Dave in his car to a bar that had outside seating and a large lot.

We parked the bus in eyeshot and, sat down and ordered drinks. He then took out a contract he was carrying in a folder and placed it on the table. He said it was a basic contract but recommended we have our lawyer look at it. A lawyer, we thought? The only lawyers we knew were the appointed councils at the county courts, but of course, we didn't mention that. He explained that he would try to help us with booking show tours and setting up live showcases for recording labels. Ultimately, it would entail staying in Austin for a while.

We mentioned the Whisky show, and he questioned whether now was the right time. His thinking was to build a better live show and record a better demo. There would be time for showcases in L.A. soon enough, and if we stayed in Austin, we could possibly earn some money and build a following. Dave paid for the drinks, said let's stay in touch, and then headed back to the office. We had a lot of hard and fast thinking to do and clearly were not in the right mind to do it.

Inside the bar was a band setting up, so we decided to order some more drinks and hung around to check it out. I desperately needed to empty my bowels and headed inside to find the head. The interior was dimly lit and had postcards, license plates, and car parts plastered all over the walls. I followed the sign that said restrooms and then pushed a thickly painted red door with the Men's sign on it and entered what looked like a scene in a nightmare. There were no urinals, just a troth and three raised toilets with no stalls around them, and only one of them had a seat. It was pretty bad in there, but still nothing compared to the pisser at CBGB's in New York, so in a way, I felt right at home. Luckily, it was dimly lit. There was no one in there at that moment, so I figured it was now or never. I stepped up onto the platform the toilets were raised on, said a little prayer to the gods of crap, dropped my pants, and reluctantly sat down. Of course, at that moment, two huge, greasy dudes with trucker hats and tattoos walked in. Damn. As soon as they saw me, they painfully turned their heads away in disgust and moved towards the troths. "Good evening, gentlemen, pleased to make your acquaintances" I said desperately trying to hide the embarrassment in my voice. It was the longest 60 seconds I had ever experienced. As they departed, they waved to me and said while laughing, "Have a great night." Fucking rock and roll.

When I left the restroom, I could see the boys were hanging at the bar while the band was setting up their gear on the floor-level stage. While walking towards them, I passed the two dudes I just met in the crapper as they sneered and gave a thumbs-up that didn't go unnoticed by the boys. "What was that about?" asked Mitch. "I just took a shit in there, and there's no stall around the toilet, and they're my witnesses." There was a huge collective "Nooooo" as they handed me the drink that I desperately needed and patted me on the back. The bar band had set up and eventually kicked into gear. We learned from the bartender that they were a group of local musicians who would get together once in a while to blow off steam from whatever their regular paying gigs were.

There was a drummer, bassist, guitarist, keys, and sax, and they were whipping up a pot of stinky jazz, funk, Mexicali, and metal that was as hilarious as it was serious.

Imagine Zappa meets The Dixie Dregs meets Los Lobos with a dash of Charlie Parker. After every song, the small but mighty crowd would go nuts, and the bartender would ring a brass bell while a tipping bucket would fly around the bar on a string and pullies hung from the ceiling. This is how the band got paid. We did our part and stuffed our dollars into the bucket. The music pulled me in, as it usually does when there are virtuoso musicians cutting it up. The boys had a different reaction. If there wasn't an image or a show or an ideology to go with the music, then it wasn't interesting enough, and if the abilities of the musician rose above their own, they seemed to have to separate themselves from it. On the other hand, I would get hypnotized by the virtuosity, as I would with an amazing surfer or martial artist. I didn't have to identify with it to absorb it.

The boys were focused on drinking, and as we kept drinking, our problems kept mounting. What were we doing? Were we going to California to play the Whisky, or were we staying in Austin to work with Dave, or maybe we would do both, do the Whisky, then come back to Austin? But we had even more immediate problems like, we were way off our spending budget and where the hell were we staying that night. But in the moment, we were partying, meeting people, enjoying live music at its best. We were on the road, dirty, tired, intoxicated, with no clue what tomorrow would bring. We were, as they say, young, dumb, and full of cum. As the bartender shouted out the last call, we ordered the final round and unanimously decided we would do the Whisky and then return to Austin. We raised our glasses and made a toast: California, here we come!

THE WEST IS THE BEST

After the bar closed, we marched back to the bus along with some of the musicians in the band and their friends as we were all wired up from the music and the sniffing powder. They told us about the Austin music scene and how hard it was for bands playing original music to gain a following, and you still had to go to L.A. to get record deals. We drank, smoked, and talked till the sun started to come up, and gradually, our talked-out, cranked-up guests finally left. We were too tired and wasted to go anywhere, so we just passed out on the bus in the empty parking lot. Hours later, when we eventually awoke, it was afternoon, hot, and the lot was bustling with cars buzzing all around us. It was pure luck that the police didn't come and kick us out or something worse.

We decided not to push that luck and pulled ourselves together and got the hell out of there. We were all looking pretty gnarly. I was totally dehydrated and definitely not feeling my best, and my long, kinky hair was starting to dreadlock from not picking out the knots every day as I usually would. Finding a truck stop where we could get some food, clean up, and make some phone calls seemed like the practical thing to do. The bus didn't start right away, but after a few alarming tries, it finally kicked over. But it definitely raised our concerns, and also, we were low on gas. We had to get organized and start focusing on the Whisky gig. Rick was struggling to drive the bus in traffic in his current state and just barely avoided several fender benders and bounced over a few curbs. We needed to get on a highway. It seemed like forever getting out of the city, but we eventually got on the highway heading west. Our plan was to pull over once we passed a place with gas, phones, food, and bathrooms and then drive into the desert.

Pulling into a truck stop always drew us lots of attention from the herds of tourists, truck drivers, and vagabonds, coming and going from their vehicles, sporting their trucker hats, stretch shorts, and American flag t-shirts, all the while carrying cans of soda, paper coffee cups, and bags of candies and chips. We pulled in like we owned the place and docked the blue demon beside a dusty gas pump, filled up the tank, added oil, cleaned the windshield, discarded trash, and filled the water cooler with a hose. Besides having to pump the brakes, the bus was enduring, better than we could say for ourselves, but probably it could use a new battery. We parked and then dragged our sorry asses to the small restaurant that was dwarfed by the infestation of cars and trucks surrounding it.

Walking through the doors of the place, we knew we must have looked like the Adam's Family on drugs and more than likely smelled like a distillery. As we strutted past the customers eating their burgers and chicken fried steaks, the curious looks continued with leering eyes following us as we collapsed into a corner booth. We kept to our routine of using the restroom one at a time so as not to draw too much attention. When it was my turn, I practically took a bath in that shabby bathroom sink. I stared at myself in the mirror for a good long while. I looked like shit with my red bloodshot eyes and the black rings underneath them. My hair was a rat's nest, and my skin tone was greenish. It was hard to tell where the party ended and the hangover began as one rolled into the other. I told myself I needed to pull it together if I was going to make it to L.A. Back at the table, we held a meeting while devouring our sandwiches and fries. We decided we would drive as far as we could go and then sleep in the desert under the stars. It would be two days before we would hit L.A. anyway, and we weren't in any rush. After staying way too long in the restaurant, we headed back to the bus. I used a payphone to call David but instead got an answering machine. I left a detailed message about our plans and told him we would call back in two or three days.

Getting back on the open road felt good, more relaxed, but the bus had been baking in the broiling sun all day and was ripe with B.O. and the stench of stale cigarette ash. I swapped the black jeans I was wearing for a pair of running shorts and took off any other clothing besides a t-shirt that I wrapped around my head like a turban, getting the long hair off my face and back. Opening the windows created a breeze but did nothing at all to simmer down the stifling heat. I fended off the urge to smoke or drink and just stared out the window, watching the green rolling hills turn into rocky plains while listening to the stereo speakers battling for dominance over the clanging outer shell of the bus. I was melting inside and out. But there was also a feeling of freedom like I was a pilgrim on the highway to hell.

As minutes turned into hours, the sky started to turn as rust-colored as the surrounding terrain. Was there a storm brewing? Rick called out from the driver's seat, "What the hell is that?" We all moved up front to look out the windshield. At first, we were all clueless, but almost like a collective consciousness, we gasped in unison, "A fucking tornado?" Holy shit, a mother fucking tornado. It was pretty far from us, but for us, being northeasterners, it was terrifying to see for the first time, and we were driving right towards it. The sky was hideously monstrous, with swirling black clouds and spider-like lightning bolts stinging the ground. Whipped up dust particles bouncing off the bus in a high-pitched sizzling din started piercing through the windows, so we quickly closed them. A thin film of brown matter layered on top of our stuff. Luckily, the tornado crossed our path far enough ahead and then started to move away from us. Eventually, we caught up to where it had crossed the highway, and we could see its violent footprints in the tangled earth and brush. The lightning lingered and sometimes came frighteningly close. We realized we were probably the tallest thing out there in this stretch of rock and stone, which didn't put us at ease. So much for a relaxing ride.

Eventually, the storm moved into the rear-view mirrors and there were patches of clear sky starting to emerge. We were entering the desert. At first, there were gullies and ridges, but eventually, the ground became flat and there was nothing but cactus and sand for miles ahead of us. The heat was relentless, and the falling sun was blazing into the windshield as we headed west. We decided to take an off-road and find a place to park for the night before it got too dark. We drove for almost a half hour without seeing another vehicle and then came across an off-ramp to nowhere, which we figured was a good a spot as any to pull into. Even though the sun was going down, it was still plenty hot. We all got out and stretched our battered bodies while observing our surroundings.

We had no idea what to look for or if it was legal or even safe to park there. What did we know, we were from New York and this was the first time any of us were ever in a desert. Shane and Rick decided to set up the camping grill they brought, and all we had were hotdogs, but that was fine with us. Mitch and I took out the acoustic guitars, sat on the ground, and played. Soon, the grill was up and burning, and the dogs were on; the beers were opening, albeit warm, but we didn't care; we loved it. We also knew we didn't belong out there, and that made it all the better. As we ate and drank our meal, the sun quickly disappeared, and the raging heat finally retreated. What a relief. Above us, the night stars began to reveal themselves until the entire Milky Way filled the massive sky. It was the most magnificent view I had ever seen. We smoked a phat joint and finished the beers. It was actually getting slightly brisk outside, so we broke down the grill and retired to the bus.

I'm not sure when I fell asleep, and I didn't know for how long, but when I woke up, I thought I was freezing to death. My toes and fingers were numb. I was colder than I'd ever been in my life and I could see my breath like it was the middle of winter. There was light inside the bus because the stars were so bright outside; they actually lit the interior. The boys were passed out. "What the fuck is going on" I whined and started to look for more clothes to put on but couldn't focus on where they would be, and then I realized my teeth had been chattering the whole time. Fuck, it was really cold.

I tried to wake up the boys with a shove and then a push, but they barely responded. I felt so heavy it was hard to move around the bus. I decided to start the engine to see if the heater worked; we had never tried it before. My fingers hurt turning the key and my foot hurt pressing the gas. It took a few turns before the engine finally came to life, "Thank God," I thought. I turned the heat on, but only freezing cold air wheezed out. It probably just needed to warm up first. I noticed several windows were opened and tried to close them, but they were hard enough to open and close without the frostbite, so I gave up.

The boys began to move slowly but they seemed in worse shape than me. I began to feel better as I moved around and was able to find the case with my clothes. I put on pants and every long sleeve shirt I had and over that, my leather jacket. The boys were awake now, but everyone's teeth were chattering. The heater never got warm. We were too fucked up, numb, and drowsy to start driving in the middle of the night, in the middle of the desert, in the middle of Texas, so I shut the engine off. We weren't in good shape. We only had one warm blanket on the bus, and we would have to get everyone close together like the penguins I once saw on an Animal Kingdom TV show when I was a kid. This was an awkwardly desperate moment. Under normal circumstances, there would be a competitive barrage of homo-erotic one-upmanship digs shot across the collective bow but no one was feeling any sense of humor at this point. Slowly and quietly, besides the chattering of teeth, we made our way to the back of the bus, grabbing anything warm to cover ourselves. It was extremely uncomfortable, but eventually, my teeth stopped chattering. It was working, and I fell into a shallow sleep.

I could hear the sound of the morning from underneath the blanket as I woke in a pile of near-frozen drunken rock and rollers. I was half awake and half comatose, but my ears could hear a bird in the distance and some sort of critters scurrying around outside the bus. My fingers and toes were no longer numb but my body hurt all over. I could no longer stay in the position I was in, so I decided to get up. I crawled out from under the blanket and could see a soft orange-gold light filtering through the windows. It was still chilly but nowhere close to what it was during the night. I made it to the couch and flopped down on it. I felt broken and filthy. I needed to soak in a hot bath for a few hours and then a serious massage but that wasn't going to happen anytime soon. The sun was rising fast, and so was the heat. I didn't know it then, but I was probably extremely dehydrated.

All of us probably were. These were the days when we drank anything but water. I grabbed a roll of toilet paper and stepped off the bus. There wasn't much brush to go behind, but I didn't care by this point; I felt like a wild animal. As I covered up the deed with dirt, the boys began limping off the bus. Passing Shane, I tossed him the roll. He looked like I felt. We didn't talk much at first, but slowly, we started to snap out of it. "That was fucked up," somebody said. The truth was we were probably embarrassed about not knowing shit about the nature of nature and that sharing our body heat under the blanket probably saved us. There were no wisecracks or sarcastic attitudes, just five extremely hung-over dudes who had a lot of driving to do. We didn't waste too much time hanging around, so we packed up camp and got ready to roll. I could already feel the heat starting to rise, and right then understood why the desert was such a beautiful, brutal place. We started up the bus and prepared ourselves for the next surprise, and we didn't have to wait long. As soon as the bus began to make its way up the pseudo ramp that we rolled down the night before, the wheels began to spin in the sand.

Damn, it was only a few feet till we would hit the pavement. There wasn't anything we could do but get out and push, and believe me, that was the last thing we wanted to do. Rick took the driver's seat because he was the best with the clutch. Luckily, the pushing worked, but we all got blasted with sand from the spinning wheels. After brushing ourselves off, we limped onto the bus, dirty and bruised but not defeated. We drove the half hour back to the main road. By this time, we were all taking turns driving the bus, at least on the highways in the middle of nowhere, and we could switch drivers mid-saddle without stopping. I swapped with Rick and settled down on the wide green pleather cushion seat, both my hands on the huge, almost flat leaning steering wheel, and pushed down on the big metal gas pedal.

The bus could only go about 55 miles per hour at the most.

Massive Mack truck tractor-trailers would fly by us and nearly blow us off the road. But besides the random tornado and occasional lightning bolts, it was mostly a peaceful time behind the wheel of the giant blue demon. The driver usually got to choose the music that was played, and for this session, I put on Lightin' Hopkins, my favorite Texas bluesman. The sound of Lightin's voice, the giant open sky, and the long stretch of road put me in a blissful state of mind. After a while, we started to pass signs for Mexico. We were driving along the border. Driving along the border back in the eighties was different than it is today. It was raw and rough. Passing by us were old rusty pickup trucks carrying junk or chickens in cages, dusty bikers riding in packs of ten, police, sheriffs, and state troopers in their Dodges and Plymouths, and flame-painted pin-striped low riders that crawled along the road like insects.

We needed gas, so we figured it was a good time to get some food and clean up a bit too. We actually passed quite a few gas stations that looked like they were from a bygone era but were mostly closed or in disarray. We were never this low on gas before with the bus so we started to get paranoid about how much reserve there was left. We came upon what looked like a small town, so we took the exit off the highway. We hoped there would be an open gas station and some decent food. The bus was actually bigger than most of the houses we passed, and more than a few seemed to be abandoned. Dilapidated cars were piled up on the brown dead lawns and so far, we only saw a couple of mangey dogs but no people. Up ahead, we saw a smudgy kid dragging what looked like bags of fertilizer on a makeshift sled with a rope.

We pulled up next to him. He was sweating in the pounding sun. I opened the doors and shouted to him, "Hola, is there a gas station in this town?" He looked at me, confused at first, and then looked at the bus. "Gasoline?" I repeated. He didn't speak; he just slowly lifted his arm, pointed his finger, and twitched his head in the same direction. "Thanks" I said and closed the door. Surprisingly, there was a gas station there, but it was hard to tell if it was open or abandoned. There were only two pumps, and they were old and greasy. I sloppily pulled the bus in and shut it down. We slipped out of the bus into the bright sun and strangling heat. There was a garage with lifts and a small office. I could see through the window there was someone inside. Anthony, Mitch, and I went in while Rick and Shane took care of fueling the bus. Inside was a very wrinkly older man sitting in front of a cash register and an ancient metal fan blowing directly on him. He was drinking something in a large Styrofoam cup with a straw.

"Hello" we said and asked if there was a restaurant in town. Just like the kid in the street, without saying anything, he lazily lifted his hand and pointed through the window. Just down the street was an old grey building with faded flags hanging from the awning and a sign outside that just read 'BAR.' We thanked the old guy, paid for the gas, and went back outside. Shane got back on the bus and drove over to the bar while the rest of us walked.

Man, it was hot. The whole town, including everything in it, looked burnt. We stepped into the bar. It was dark inside, with no light coming in from the outside. There was a long wooden bar with stools and eight or so tables. The tables were empty, but sitting at the bar were several sweaty dudes with their backs towards us at first, but they turned around to look right at us as we walked in.

The bartender was a weathered, portly woman with a bandanna wrapped around her head. It definitely smelled like beer and fried oil, and the air conditioner was as loud as the Mexican music squeaking out of a single old box speaker hanging from the ceiling. There was a kitchen in the back behind swinging doors that had fluorescent light escaping through two round portholes casting shadows on a well-worn pool table. The bartender raised her voice and, in a strong Mexican accent, said, "Can I help you?" "Is the kitchen open?" I answered. She nodded, grabbed some menus, and lifted them up to signal for us to take them. I went to grab them and asked if it was ok to put a couple of tables together. She nodded yes. I glanced over at the patrons at the bar, and they raised their glasses in recognition. I nodded back, took the menus, and walked back to the boys, who were putting the tables together. We were hungry. The menu had most things crossed off, but they had tacos and Dos Equis, so I went with that. The Bartender came over and took our order.

Nature was calling, so I went to the restroom, which was as bad as the one in Austin, but at least it had stalls. My digestion was definitely taking a hit from too much alcohol and not eating properly, but I didn't necessarily put those things together at that time, and I just thought maybe I caught a bug. The food came, and it actually wasn't that bad. The cooks came from right over the border so they knew how to do a lot with a little. The tortillas and salsa were freshly made, and the chorizo and carnitas were spicey hot and it all washed down perfectly with the ice-cold beers. We ordered more of everything. The bartender gave us a round of homebrew tequila shots on the house. It was like rocket fuel but slightly more delicious. One of the characters sitting at the bar came over to us and asked if we needed anything, and he repeated, as in 'anything.' We asked him, "Whada'ya got?" He motioned to sit down with us, and we motioned back. He grabbed a chair and leaned in towards us to say, "I got Smack, Crack, Crank, Coke, Acid, Masculine, PCP, and weed." Each of us had that single raised eyebrow look. He continued, "I also have pistols, rifles, knives, dynamite, and plastic explosives." Now, our other eyebrow went up. He continued, "I can also get pussy, cock, mouth, ass, tranny, you name it." Sean didn't miss a beat and said with a gleam in his eyes, "Well, we definitely came to the right place!" and we all busted out laughing. We ordered another round of tequilas and expressed that we would pass on the human trafficking and weapons, but we would definitely be interested in sampling the assortment of party favors he would have in his possession. We told him we would pay the bill and meet him at the big blue bus out front. He left to get what I assumed was his stash, and we asked for the check, which was super cheap. We loved this place. We headed back outside into the dust and heat. We stood around smoking cigarettes until the guy came out and all the patrons and the bartender were following him. They were all curious about us and the bus. Turns out they were all slightly related to each other, cousins, with a combination of indigenous, Mexican, and European blood.

We figured out the bar was just a front for bringing things and people across the border. A part of me worried if we were being too vulnerable and exposed to someone clearly involved in illegal activity, but then I thought, so were we most of the time. We let them on the bus and told them our story, which they loved, and everybody started loosening up a little. On the bus, we had started to use Anthony's kick drum case as a coffee table where our new friend had laid out his smorgasbord of party favors on top. The weed wasn't the best, but he gave us a great price. The coke too, was pretty stepped on, but we went for it. I would have been interested in the Acid, but there was no way to test it, so I passed. They were very interested in the bus and wanted to know how

149

and where we got it, and then that broke off into all of us having separate conversations, and it became a hangout.

After a while, more people started passing by, and we rotated in and out of the bus. Some people were going into the bar and then came back outside with their beers, so one by one, we went back in and came out with beers too. We figured at this point, with more people hanging around, it was better not to leave the bus alone and some of the new folks that started to hang around had a much darker energy. After a while, we figured out that they were junkies looking to score. There was a hint of danger in the air. It was probably best for us to move on. A couple of gang-banger-type characters seemed to sense our anxiousness and tried to convince us not to leave and to go back to the bar, but when we said no thank you, they started to get angry. A couple of them were lifting up their shirts, exposing the back end of the guns stuffed into their pants. Luckily the bartender seemed to be the matriarch of the mob and got them to chill out.

We took advantage of the moment and quickly got on the bus. Rick started it up, backed it out, and we left the same way we came; meanwhile, we were looking out the back window to see if we were being followed but we kicked up so much dust it was hard to tell. We got back on the highway a lot later than we had planned, and again, feeling like we dodged some more bullets. Being far from sober, we contemplated where to crash for the night. We were seeing signs for El Paso and agreed to head there to check it out and maybe find a cheap motel. Traffic was definitely building, and we got the feeling we were moving towards a big city. In my head, I pictured El Paso as a 'Wild West', 'Gunfight at the OK Corral' kind of place, but in actuality, it's a massive border town that's basically the sister city to Ciudad Juarez across the border in Mexico, and combined, the two are populated with well over a million people, mostly Hispanic or Latino.

As in New York, the bus stood out like a sore thumb in the sprawling urban vista and there were cops and military vehicles everywhere. We figured we might as well drive right through the city just to get some bearings and a feel for the place. Rick popped out of the driver's seat, and I took over. The city was mostly flat with low mountains dividing the city into two halves and a downtown area down by the Rio Grande River. A lot of the city looked modern and clean, but we passed tent cities on the side of the road the closer to the border we got. We also passed a lot of cool, old-school motels with tall, funky neon signs, but we were holding out for one where the bus didn't take up the entire parking lot.

After baking in the heat all day then freezing during the night, and then another day baking, I was fried. My stomach still wasn't great, and I was filthy. My lungs were singed from smoking, my liver was sore from drinking, and my skin was dried out from dehydration and exposure, and there was a lingering feeling of anxiety from having to do it all over again. It isn't easy not to join in the celebration of being in a new place and meeting new people. I was also afraid it was a sign of weakness, a lack of faith in the gods of rock and roll. We made it to the west side of the city, and I took us off the main highway. It was the first time I was driving in a big city with a bus, and the intersection was a bit confusing, and I may have cut off a couple of cars by accident.

Almost instantly, flashing lights bounced off the inside of the bus. Two short siren bursts cut through the sound system. We were being pulled over. I quickly turned the music down, and the boys hid any exposed empties and paraphernalia. Downshifting the bus quickly was not an easy move for a novice, not to mention having to navigate and actually stop the bus on the side of the road; all the while, a cop car was up our ass. This sucked. Eventually, I docked the ship, opened the door, and got my license and registration ready. I watched in the large bus review mirrors; one cop stayed in the car while the other got out and walked very slowly beside the bus, even bending down to look underneath it.

The adrenalin pumping through my veins removed all of my hangover symptoms, but I suddenly became conscious of what I looked like. I had my huge curly hair that was starting to turn into dreadlocks, exploding out of a green t-shirt which I wrapped around my head, making it look like an alien turban with a black palm tree growing out of it, and I was basically naked besides sandals and a pair of ripped to shreds shorts, something like what a castaway would be wearing after being shipwrecked on a deserted island. To top it all off, I had on my favorite oversized round mirrored sunglasses. With the shades, green t-shirt, and hair, I looked like a giant bug, a punk rock praying mantis. As I waited for the cop to reach the door, I turned and looked back at the wide-eyed delinquent young lads lurking in the mayhem interior of the bus, "Jesus," I thought, "we're fucked." The cop was young, around my age, maybe a few years older. Upon reaching the entrance he stood still for an awkward moment as he took in the vision that was me. His facial expression was a mixture of confusion and concern.

In the absence of any words, I simply said, "Hi," and slowly waved my hand. He responded in a tone of disbelief, "License and registration, please."

and reached out his hand. I got out of the driver's seat and handed the cop the documents and moved right back to the seat. He briefly looked them both over then said, "Ok, please stay where you are," and then walked back to the car and the other officer. As we were waiting, another cop car pulled up in front of us, boxing us in. But this one said border control on the side of the car door. The first cop walked over to it, holding my license in his hand as two border patrol officers stepped out. They were speaking, looking at the bus, and looking at my license. All three officers walked up to the bus entrance. The cop who took my I.D. said, "Ok, what's the deal here?" I took a deep breath, turned, looked back at the boys, and said, "We're a band from New York on our way to play a gig in Los Angeles." The cop then took his turn, taking a deep breath, and said, "If everyone would please step out of the vehicle and have your I.D.s available, then these gentlemen would enter the vehicle for an inspection."

Fuck, this was not good. We all piled out and handed over our I.D.s. Luckily, we all got our driver's licenses up to date before we left New York. One of the immigration cops took our I.D.s back to their car, and the other one boarded the bus. We had a ton of fuckery on the bus, but it was very well hidden inside the gear, but the shit we scored in the previous town was just thrown under the disgusting couch. I could see the cop through the windows looking around the bus, but he didn't seem to be touching anything. He was probably too grossed out. These cops were super clean-cut, way more so than New York City cops. Their uniforms were pressed, their hair was cut super short, and even their nails looked manicured.

He did lean over the barricade at the back of the bus looking for whatever. Then he turned around and stepped out of the bus. "Open the back door." He ordered, and I obliged. I swung the door open, and you could clearly see amps, speakers, guitars, and drums, obviously musical gear with a big crappy mattress on top of it. Then he said, "Thank you, you can close it." and walked right passed us towards his car with his partner in it, checking our I.D.s. We all stood there on the side of the road, our fate in the hands of these three men. After what seemed like an eternity, the immigration cop walked over to the first cop, nodded, and then handed him our licenses. Then, the first cop handed all the licenses to me and barked, "Good luck on your show in California; I highly recommend you continue on your journey now. Get back onto this road, look for the highway sign saying west, and just keep going. Good day, gentleman." And that was it, they got back in their cars and drove away. I nearly collapsed right there in the street. We all breathed a huge sigh of relief, and I handed back everyone's licenses and also handed Rick the keys; there was no way I was going to get behind that wheel; I was a mess. Anyway, that was close, to say the least, so much for checking out El Paso. We were just a few miles from the New Mexico border. It was time to get the hell out of Dodge.

Those cops pulled us over to see if we were trafficking humans. It was a harsh dose of reality for us northern boys to swallow. We entered New Mexico exhausted and grateful, but there was also a whole lot of nothing. We drove for about an hour and a half till we came across what was barely a town, but they had a motel with ample parking for the bus, and at this point, we just needed a place to chill, a shower, and hopefully something edible. We pulled in front of the office of some generic motel that had not one single living plant in its vicinity. There was nothing but burnt reddish-brown dirt for miles around. Sitting at portable tables in the roasting parking lot were three very serious-looking women of various ages that I would guess as indigenous, selling handmade jewelry.

I got off the bus and walked into the building. Inside was a simple motel registration desk, an extremely modest gift shop, and a breakfast café area with a coffee maker, teapot, and plastic cups, plates, and utensils. I handed the clerk my credit card and got us a ground-floor double that we could park the bus right in front of. We pulled the bus around, parked, and escaped for the sanctuary of the room. The first thing we did was crank the air conditioner, but like the room, it wasn't that cool. Between the heat, the hangovers, and the cops, morale was at a low point. I was definitely running the credit card up on gas, rooms, food, and drink, but at the moment, I didn't care. I just wanted to shower and sleep. Even the barrage of farts and burps going on didn't affect me. The boys took a smoke break, and I hit the shower. Looking at myself in the bathroom mirror, I tried to run a pick and a brush through my knotted hair, but it was no use.

If I didn't consistently manage my curls, the ends would dread, and then the dreads would lock together, creating a nappy mess. I either went with it, which meant I had to help it along by rolling the locks in my hands for at least an hour a day or cut them out, which usually meant a total haircut. Wrapping my hair in a t-shirt probably wasn't helping. I was tempted to cut it all off, but I knew it would be an issue with the band. In the eighties, many famous musicians started to cut the hair that they once wore long in the 60s and 70s to fit in with the cleaner-cut new wave pop stars. Heavy rockers like ourselves resisted the impulse to follow the fashion of the day. The irony was Mitch, Anthony, and Shane all had shorter hair when I met them, but I'd been wearing my hair past my shoulders since I was a kid. I had older brothers who had long hair, and I would argue, mostly with my dad, that if they could have it, why couldn't I?

I understand now my dad's apprehension then because back in the day, males with long hair risked having violence acted on them by xenophobes, homophobes, nationalists, religious zealots, and your basic run-of-the-mill assholes, so long hair was like a badge of honor, plus chicks dug it! Anyway, there was nothing I could do about it at that moment, so it was motel shampoo, rinse, repeat. After we all got cleaned up as much as we could, we then watched the sun go down dramatically in the desert sky, and our collective mood changed. We were excited about possibly making it to Los Angeles the next day if nothing else got in our way. We hid the contraband we picked up in Texas, mapped out our final journey, and organized and cleaned the garbage out of the bus. We needed to do laundry desperately, but we were too burned out to deal with it. We all took turns using the payphone. I tried to call a few more clubs in LA but was having no luck getting anyone to pick up. About our daily party ritual, it seemed everyone was taking a break from the substance abuse for the night.

They probably felt as destroyed as I did, and besides the occasional car passing by, it was quite serene where we were. The energy in the air seemed different than Texas, perhaps more peaceful. I wasn't sure, but it felt good to chill for a while. Anthony and Mitch stayed up watching TV, so I took the couch and passed out. Shane and Rick hung out on the bus. I believe the bouncing around inside the moving bus and the constant banging of every bump and dip in the road exasperated the insomnia and hangovers because the next day, I felt like a new man after sleeping in a quiet room that wasn't barreling down a highway. We all woke up early and hungry. Over at the motel cafe, breakfast was drip coffee, a big box of cornflakes, milk, wonder bread, margarine, and little packets of grape jellies. We decided to take advantage of the empty calories so we could drive as far as we could without stopping. After breakfast, we filled the ice bucket and threw some beers into it. Because the bus was only capable of slow speed, it would probably take fourteen or fifteen hours to get to L.A. Anthony volunteered the first shift of driving and the rest of us took our places. We had passed the threshold of the southwest. West Coast, here we come.

GOLD IN THEM THAR HILLS

When most people talk about the history of the United States, they often speak of The Colonies, The American Revolution, or The Civil War, but the story less told is that of the gold rush, when people from all over the planet left their families, their cultures, and everything they owned, to come to the American frontier and claim their fortunes. In many ways, that frontier had finally been tamed by the beginning of the 21st century. Now, the West is everywhere, and slowly but surely, the world is beginning to drift back east, but in the late eighties, California, and especially Los Angeles, was still the wild west and we were prospectors of rock and roll. We drove towards Tucson and then through Phoenix. As I sat in my seat staring out the window, I started to hear melodies and riffs playing in my head, but the constant banging of the bus and Anthony blasting Hanoi Rocks out of the speakers made it hard to concentrate, but I knew songs were coming. I've always heard tunes in my head ever since I was a kid.

At first, I just listened to them as if it were a record or a radio station. Then, after a while, I started remembering them and would hum along. Being a kid, I didn't realize not everyone heard music in their head, and as I matured, the internal sound got louder and louder, to the point where when the muse was calling, it got difficult to focus on anything else in my life. As a teenager, I would record a beat on my drum set on an old school cassette recorder and then, with a second recorder, hum along to the drum playback from the first recorder and overdub back and forth just using my voice and drums. That's how I started to record songs.

When I started to play with bands, if the guitarist, bassist, or keyboardist left their instruments behind, I would take advantage of it and try to figure out how to play the parts I heard in my head. That's how I self-taught myself music. I think I may have been too embarrassed or scared to take lessons or ask for help. I was afraid someone would say that I wasn't good enough or I had no talent because deep down inside, I would have agreed with them. I knew who Miles Davis was, John Coltrane, Jimi Hendrix, and Ginger Baker, and I knew I'd never come close to that, but I could hear the notes of the songs in my head so clearly; I just had to find out how to play them. Interestingly, being in the desert sort of clarified my thoughts, and I could let my mind wander in a way I had not experienced up until that moment. In the Northeast, everyone and everything is right on top of you. Congested streets, buildings, traffic, trains, plains, parks, and people are everywhere, and nature is pushed way into the background. Silence doesn't exist. But I could feel the silence in the desert even though I was in a giant can of din rolling down the highway. I felt my mind was in contrast to the openness of the desert. My mind was like a cluttered studio apartment or a rush hour traffic jam, and the vastness of the desert slowly dissolved into dust and then into silence, disappearing into the wild blue yonder.

After driving for about four hours, we reached Tucson, and instead of investigating, we decided to just get gas, clean the windshield, stretch a bit, and then move on. We did our truck stop routine of snacks, beers, and some light shoplifting, and we were still drawing attention to ourselves every time we got off the bus, but now, we started to look like central casting for a Mad Max movie as our New York alabaster skin started to have patches of color from the sun coming through the windows and everything we owned and wore had dust all over it. We jumped back on the bus, headed out to the highway, and didn't stop till we hit Phoenix. It was mid-afternoon when we arrived just outside of town, and it was hellish hot. Even Shane had shorts on, which was a first because his body was two different colors: his top half was a kind of pinkish rose color, and his legs were a greenish postmortem white. We desperately needed a break from the heat, so we pulled into an old school diner that had a nice size parking lot and seemed quite popular with all the traffic coming in and out of it.

We caused a bit of chaos parking because the length of the bus didn't fit in the lot, so we had to back it up a few times, but eventually, we settled in.

Walking into the place, the air conditioner hit me like an iceberg. I got the feeling that the hostess seated us all the way in the back so that no one coming in the door would see us. A long-legged buxom waitress late twenties, wearing a tight short skirt uniform, came to take our order. She had big blue eyes, too much makeup, tattoos of roses and skulls, and long blue-black dyed hair pulled back tightly in a ponytail. She had a big smile for us and, in a devilish growl, said, "Well, hi there, boys, I'm Noelle; where y'all from?" We introduced ourselves and as it turned out, she hung with a local metal band called Surgical Steel and grabbed us a flyer for their show along with our menus.

We thanked her and watched her walk from our table to the next. She looked like a lot of fun. The food came quickly. While we ate, we discussed where to go next since we still had time before we had to get to LA. Shane mentioned that Joshua Tree National Park was on the way and that this time, we could prepare and stay in the desert at night without freezing to death. We agreed. After we finished eating, we would drive to town, pick up some blankets or sleeping bags, and maybe check out that gig. When Noelle brought us the check, we asked where we could do some shopping and mentioned that we were traveling on a huge school bus. She drew directions on a napkin to a nearby mall and then reminded us to make sure we came to the show by pressing the napkin against her lips, leaving a deep red lipstick signature and making it impossible for us to refuse. That's 1980's metal band street marketing for you. We headed out into the heat, slightly refreshed and definitely inspired. Back on the bus, I handed Rick the lipsticked napkin as he took the wheel, and we were shopping mall-bound.

Shopping malls in the 1980s transformed the American suburban landscape. Before malls, people shopped and ate at mom-and-pop stores and restaurants, and they would corral around towns and business centers where people lived and worked. But when the malls came, people drove in droves to once desolate out-of-the-way locations that would get converted into massive parking lots with rows of franchised chain stores owned by global corporate brands. Everyone, young, old, rich, poor, hung out at the mall. American culture became corporate culture as millions of Americans bought in and sold out to massive, air-conditioned, sterile, florescent-lit consumer castles, where you could buy a pair of Levi's, get your ears pierced, shop for furniture, and eat ice cream, all in one place.

Nowadays, everywhere is like a mall, but back then, they were novelle and suspicious. As we pulled into the vast parking lot, our massive, dusty, prison blue whale was clearly an anomaly. Rick stayed behind with the bus to stand guard as the rest of us headed inside. As we walked through the huge high-ceiling corridors, we must have looked like barbarians with our long-dyed hair, cruddy ripped-up black jeans, stained t-shirts, tattered Converse sneakers, and worn thin combat boots. In contrast, the local patrons wore lots of pastel polyester, polo shirts tucked in, skinny brown belts, and most interestingly, on girls, woolen leg warmers. Everyone was pretty much wearing the same articles we saw on the mannequins in the windows of the clothing stores we were walking by. We passed a record store that had a poster on the window of the show Noelle the waitress invited us to, and inside was a headshop where we bought loose tobacco, rolling papers, and cigarette lighters.

Eventually, we found a sporting goods store and purchased sleeping bags, torches, batteries, and a case of wet wipes. Heading back, we passed a liquor store and scored a bottle of tequila, a little something to give to Rick for being on guard duty, and to give the Jack Danielle's a break. Walking out of the mall was like stepping out of a giant refrigerator into a frying pan. It was still broiling hot even though the sun was going down as we marched back to the bus with our supplies. We found Rick shirtless, sweaty, and drinking a beer with some folks who parked next to us with their RV. They were driving from Illinois, headed to Joshua Tree. They had a campsite reserved but still had a good five or six hours till they would get there. We said our goodbyes and got on the bus. We knew it would be too late to drive all the way to Joshua Tree afterward if we went to the show. We voted unanimously to go to the show, but only to check out the band and the venue, and to stay sober, then drive as far as we could, and then park somewhere and rest. Man, we were so good at lying to ourselves.

The club was called The Mason Jar, and the line waiting to get in was packed with local metal kids; both males and females were wearing spandex, eyeliner, and hair spray, obviously parroting the L.A. scene. We parked and I volunteered to hang back with the bus on guard duty. Rick offered to switch me out after a while since it wasn't really his scene anyway, so I agreed. They headed into the show, and I pulled out my guitar and got to work. After what felt like a half hour, I heard tapping at the bus door. I put the guitar down and went and looked thru the glass. It was Noelle with another very attractive young lady beside her. They were both covered in matching torn fishnet and not much else, and they we holding hands. Totally surprised, I opened the door. "Mind if we come in," she said in that raspy voice. "Of course," I replied and led them in. By their slow, languid movements, I guessed that they were probably on something. Not drunk, but definitely very, very high. "We bumped into your friends inside the club, and they told us you were out here, and we were so curious about what you could be doing out here all by yourself." She said as they both kept touching each other's body in a strange petting motion.

"Why don't you come closer to us?" she whispered and pulled me into their slow-motion dance. I put my hands on both of their bodies, and then a slight recollection of what happened the last time I was in this situation popped into my head, and I looked around as if someone was going to barge in on us and shoot me. The two of them started kissing, and then they both started kissing me. I felt my belt unbuckling, and then I was only kissing Noelle while her friend got on her knees. Then Noelle also went to her knees, and the world outside me disappeared. They were like two kids sharing an ice cream cone for the first time. It took all my concentration not to have it all come to an end too soon, but eventually, the damn broke, and the two of them looked like they were in a pie-eating contest as they both took turns licking me off each other's faces. Then they both stood up, kissed me on the lips, held each other's hands again, and walked off the bus as mysteriously as they entered.

I couldn't believe what had just happened and stood there with my pants down for a minute, unable to move. Time stood still, and I was everywhere and nowhere at the same time. Then, the sounds outside the bus came back to me and it was like I came out of a trance. I got dressed, closed the bus door, and then just sat on the couch, feeling strangely aware of the present moment as if there was someone on the bus with me. I couldn't see them, but I could feel it. I stared at the guitar lying on the couch, picked it up, and got back to work. Eventually, Rick returned to relieve me of guard duty. I asked him if he saw Noelle inside, which he did, and he told me how she was making out at the bar with a girl dressed identically as her. I was almost afraid to go in and have it altered, in any way, the perfect experience I had, and I had no idea how to explain it to Rick at that moment. He seemed to notice my hesitation and asked, "Are you going in?" I nodded yes, lit a cigarette, and hopped off the bus towards the club.

There wasn't a line into the club anymore, and I could clearly hear the band from outside. I showed the bouncer my ID, gave the door girl five dollars, and I was in. Besides the bright lights on the stage, the club was dimly lit on the inside, and the P.A. was friggin' loud. The packed crowd was digging the band, who were, if nothing else, high energy. I kept my eyes open for Noelle but hadn't seen her yet, and Mitch, Anthony, and Shane were nowhere in sight. I walked around the club and saw a door towards the back that people were coming in and out of. It led to an outside hang-out area with people spread out everywhere and everyone there was touching and hugging and massaging and kissing. What the hell was going on here? Then, out of nowhere, a dude with really long hair pulled back into a ponytail, baggy oversized clothes, and the same expression on his face Noelle and her friend had on the bus asked me if I wanted any Ecstasy. I stopped for a second, thought, and then asked him, "Ecstasy?" He opened his hand and had a small plastic baggie filled with little round pills. "One for $10, two for $15," he slurred. At that point, I wondered if that was what Noelle was on. Before that moment, I had never heard of it.

I asked if he was hanging around for a while. He said he might but couldn't guarantee the pills would. I hesitated on the purchase. My fear at the time was that it may have been an opiate of some sort, and I made a promise to myself that I would never again do any opiates. When I was sixteen, I smoked opium, and it scared the shit out of me how much I liked it. That little voice in my head told me, "This is very dangerous for you." For some reason, I heeded that inner voice but many of my friends through the years weren't so lucky. I've watched heroin transform people I knew into complete strangers and super talented or charming beings into zombies, and in the end, wind up either in jail or dead. I recognized within myself that attraction of numbing all the pain and anxiety of daily life and just saying fuck it all with a fix. But I observed in others that feeling doesn't last long, and after a while, it just becomes chasing a dragon you can never catch, and then the dragon starts to chase you. Just another grind added to the daily bullshit of existence.

Luckily for me, music, travel, and meeting people gave me the high I needed, albeit, sometimes, with a little inspiration thrown in. A few years after this trip, I would discover the damage alcohol had on my body, but that's another story. I walked through the doors back into the club and circled back around, looking for my band. I found them in a dark corner, drinking and smoking and hitting on a bunch of metal chicks. It was a beautiful sight; they looked happy. I didn't want to alter the dynamic they seemed to have going so I went to watch the band for a while. The band had everything an 80s metal band had to have, like long teased hair-sprayed locks, shiny tight spandex clothing, full makeup like eye shadow, rouge, and lipstick, Charvel guitars with whammy bars, strapped up real high, and played fast in the finger tapping style of Eddie Van Halen, double kick drums, trebly bass guitar usually following what the guitar plays or one single pumping note, and male vocals singing in a female vocal range.

The songs were kind of dumb and anti-intellectual, usually arranged with the chorus at the top of the song, sung in a gang-style vocal that the audience can shout along with. As good as the band was at all this, I personally couldn't hang with the aesthetic. I get why the teased hair, spandex, and makeup, so you'd stand out in a crowd, but if everyone is doing it, doesn't it defeat the purpose? And I was never a fan of the 80s breed of guitars like Charvel's or Kramer's. I didn't like the sound or feel or look of them. I preferred guitars from the 40's, 50's, and 60s, and the only Eddie Van Halen style guitarist I liked was Eddie Van Halen. Post EVH, rock guitarists became stunt guitarists, meaning the more athletic you played was more important than how emotional you played. I never acquired a taste for it, and the same with post Van Halen West Coast rock bass players, who, instead of supporting the melody and harmony, chose to play a monotone note for the stunt guitarists to do finger gymnastics over.

Equally histrionic were the vocalists who sang in a falsetto or head voice that usually resulted in a shriek more than a melody. Naturally, I felt out of place, and this new rock music was moving in a direction I wasn't getting into. There was a plus, though, with this scene, which was this image attracted a lot of female fans who were very open sexually. They really appreciated the performance and energy that the musicians gave on stage, and they showed their appreciation generously and the dudes that played this music knew it and clearly took advantage. It was an interesting symbiosis of bubblegum pop and heavy rock. The whole time I was watching the band, I was looking for Noelle, but there was no sign of her.

I kept reimagining the scene with her and her friend on the bus, and now she was nowhere in sight. It wasn't easy purposely avoiding getting intoxicated, and I suddenly felt lost and far from home, completely unprepared for what may happen next, and oddly enough, I was enjoying it. Turning around, I left the club and headed back to the bus to check up on Rick. When I got outside, there was a raucous going on in the parking lot. It looked like two different groups antagonizing each other. One group looked like the kids in the club, while the other looked more hardcore thrash biker metal, meaning more macho, dirty, and uglier. More people came out of the club and joined in. Someone must have gone back for reinforcements. The bus, as usual, was parked towards the back of the lot, which meant I had to make my way around the rumble as more and more kids gathered around, instigating the fight. I got past them and could see Rick outside the bus holding the sword and monitoring the situation.

When I reached him, I asked if he knew what was going on. He said, "Some dude was trying to get this girl to leave with him, but she didn't want to," and at that moment, I saw Noelle at the center of the crowd, looking totally twisted but being protected from the troll looking dudes by who I assumed were her friends. "That's Noelle, the waitress from the diner!" I said and moved towards her. The trolls saw me coming from behind them and turned towards me. Up close, they looked totally jacked on something, like crackheads. "Leave her alone!" I said, and at that moment, a bottle thrown from the crowd slammed into one of the troll's heads, and the battle was on. I ran into it to get Nicolle out of there, and Rick followed me keeping idiots at bay with the sword. Fists were flying everywhere as we pulled her out and brought her to the bus.

She was totally out of it. Then the crowd turned on us, yelling as if we were trying to kidnap her. Rick looked at me and said, "This ain't good." Luckily, a few people recognized we weren't with the trolls and saved us. Then, in the distance came the sound of sirens. The whole parking lot scattered like cockroaches. Some people ran towards the club, others towards their cars. I could hear all the engines starting at the same time, like at the start of a race. Dust and fumes filled the air. Noelle disappeared with her friends into the dense cloud while Mitch, Shane, and Anthony popped out of it. "What the hell?" they said in unison. "Get in!" ordered Rick, pointing at the bus. We all got in, and Rick started it up, but it was too late. Several police cars with lights and sirens blazing came barreling into the parking lot and blocked all the exits.

Cars that were trying to leave started to lean on their horns, and with the sirens going, it sounded like New Orleans Carnival. We decided to stay put, and made sure all contraband was secure. The cops got out of their cars, with some of them holding shotguns. Turned out that the club was known to have violence, so the cops were always close by on busy nights. They quickly set up a roadblock checkpoint and began funneling cars through and checking I.D.s while shining flashlights into the vehicles. Two officers began sweeping through the parking lot. It clearly looked like they'd done this many times before. "Here we go again," said Rick. As expected, there was a tap at the door. Rick pulled the door handle, revealing a short, stocky police officer.

"Good evening," he said politely, "We got a call about an altercation, and we're asking everyone with their vehicles to make their way to the checkpoint, where you will be asked some questions and have your identification checked. Ok?" "Yes," Rick replied, and the cop moved to the next vehicle. After a while, things calmed down. The club began to empty out and cars were exiting the lot. We were hoping the police would leave before we did, but it looked like they were going to stay till the last person left, so Rick started up the bus, and we made our way towards the exit. It was no surprise when the cops took our I.D.s, quickly poked the flashlight inside the bus, asked us where we were headed, and when we answered to L.A., they let us go, recommending, of course, that we continue on our way. We recognized the pattern. So once again, we headed into the night, highway-bound, to drive as far as we could and, hopefully, find a place where we could rest. But overall, a pretty fun night!

We drove for over two hours ending up near the Arizona/California border when we saw a free campsite and pulled in. We probably disturbed the several campers and RVs that were already parked there by arriving in the middle of the night with a big noisy bus clumsily finding a spot to park, but once we did and shut the engine off, there wasn't any sound at all. Instead, there was only a deafening silence. We all had to relieve ourselves, so one by one, we took the flashlight and walked into the desert. I could feel the eyes peeking out the other vehicle windows, but I was too tired to care. It was chilly but not dark. The stars were so miraculously bright I could see the entire Milky Way as if it were five feet in front of me. I found a bush, and prayed that some snake or a spider didn't bite me. In the morning, I was awakened by the sounds of voices. I could hear children and their parents and doors opening and closing, electronic beeps and motors starting and every once in a while, a car or a truck passing quickly by.

I longed for the silence of the night before. I probably only slept for a couple of hours because it felt early, and we arrived very late, and as usual, I was the only one awake. I fell asleep on one of the bus seats with my clothes on which is not at all comfortable, so I decided I might as well get up. I looked for my sunglasses, then popped the door open and stepped out. The sun was blaring, but it wasn't roasting hot yet. There was nothing but desert all around us. I decided to go back on the bus and grab a guitar. I found a slight gully to sit by and got back to working on some of the songs rattling around in my head. Hearing the guitar and my voice bounce back at me from the gully added to the experience of being out in nature and playing music, something that in New York is much more difficult to do because there are people and sounds everywhere. It must have been a couple of hours before the boys started to crawl out of the bus. The heat was on the rise, and I could feel a slight singe on my skin. I had several songs outlined that just needed words. I headed back towards the bus. California, here we come.

After driving for about two hours, we saw our first Joshua Tree. It brought a smile to my face. I was grateful for being able to make it this far, and I found the natural beauty of the land comforting and inspiring, but it was easy to see that my comrades were anxious and impatient. They were done with the heat, dust, and vastness of the West and were ready to get back into the trash and glamour of a big city. Driving through the park, we stopped here and there to snap a couple of pics with a disposable camera until we finally rolled into the tiny town of Joshua Tree. It was getting hotter than hell out there so we stopped for snacks and drinks at a funky bar café and to wash up as much as we could before we began the climb over the San Gabriel Mountains. The cafe was just opening, so we were the first and only customers. Up front by the register were several brochures and flyers of events and tourist attractions happening in the area. We put a couple of tables together by the window to keep an eye on the bus. We got a couple of pitchers of margaritas and an order of Nachos for the table. We were only a few hours away from our destination and were in a celebratory mood. Our food and drinks were served, and we dived right in.

People started to stroll into the café. They all seemed to know each other, even waving to us as if we were at a family function. After the food was finished, we ordered another pitcher of Margaritas. We were getting buzzed. An old guy, very tan and very wrinkled, came over to our table and asked if we were coming or going, which opened up a conversation that other patrons joined in. We talked about L.A. and New York and about U2s latest album at the time, 'The Joshua Tree,' which, funny enough, the locals didn't seem to appreciate, and none of us could guess it would become one of the biggest records of all time. It felt more like we were in someone's home than a place of business. I would have liked to stay longer, maybe a night or two but my rock and roll brothers were getting anxious to move on, and perhaps the sooner we got there, the better prepared we would be. Either way, I knew it was the end of one trip and the beginning of another.

Back on the highway with Joshua Tree behind us, the mountains came into view on the horizon, and it was beautiful, but the positive experience didn't last long. As the bus started to make the slow climb up, we could feel the strain on the engine. Since we had taken the southern route across the states, this was the first time we would do any serious uphill driving with the bus, and now I was thinking, what the hell was I thinking? On flat ground, the bus could do 55 miles per hour at the most, but as we started the climb, we began to go slower and slower as the sides of the road were getting steeper and steeper. Cars and trucks were flying past us, with the big trucks pulling us into their wake and causing the bus to rock back and forth. Then, the traffic began to build behind us as we slowed down even more. People began honking their horns, both in support and annoyance, as they passed us by. We panicked that the bus could stall right there on the highway making for an extremely difficult situation. Rick shifted the bus down to its lowest gear and the engine's high pitch whine sounded like the way my nervous system felt, about to break.

The climb kept getting higher and higher, and then I remembered a children's book I read when I was a kid called 'The Little Engine That Could.' I hadn't thought about that book in so many years but in that moment, I could remember it so clearly, especially the feeling I had when I first read the story, and now it felt like I was in the story. I began to cheer the bus on, and then my comrades joined in with me. "Go, go, go, go," we shouted while Rick had his foot pressing the accelerator down to the floor, the pedal to the metal, literally. The engine was screaming, the bus was shaking, and we were barely moving, but we could see the top of the mountain. The bus breaking down there would have been a disaster. I remember saying to myself, if there are things such as miracles, we need one now! I didn't know who I was saying that to, but I felt someone or something was there, and I'm guessing that's who I was saying it to. Cars were honking their horns all around us because we were slowing the whole highway down. In my head, I had imagined we were coming through a birth canal to be reborn in the City of Angeles. "Push! Push! Push!" As we reached the peak, it felt like we were coming to the top of a rollercoaster just before it went whipping down the tracks. The bus engine was screaming in pain when we began to level out, and all of us cheered out loud. We were no longer the same people we were when we left New York. Now we were pilgrims, prospectors, pirates, the Americans coming over the mountains.

John 'Sully' Sullivan

BRIGHT LIGHTS, BIG CITY

Coming down the hills into the valley was anti-climactic. We were stuck in a massive traffic jam; it was hot, and the car fumes were overwhelming. The urban sprawl unfolded before us, and we didn't know where to go besides the Whisky or perhaps Venice Beach. None of us knew anyone in L.A., but we figured we would figure it out. We wanted to get off the highway, but to where? There was nothing recognizable on the map. We decided to go straight to Hollywood Boulevard and then take it from there. One odd thing we did notice right away was that drivers were quite aggressive, bullying for lanes and honking horns when there was nowhere to go. There were cops at the exits, cops on motorcycles weaving through the traffic, and in helicopters crisscrossing the hazy sky. After barely moving a mile in an hour we finally got off the highway, but that just slightly improved our situation. The streets were so narrow we literally had to pass certain turns because the bus didn't fit into the intersections.

Eventually we got onto a main road and finally started to make some headway. The air quality was horrendous, and so many roadside businesses looked run down or closed. It was a disorienting feeling being back in a major metropolis with cars and people everywhere, minus the skyscrapers and tension bridges. I believe it was Quentin Crisp who said, "Los Angeles is just New York lying down." We had to admit that we were totally lost, but after what seemed like randomly driving around, we just rolled right onto Sunset Boulevard. We had no idea if we were going in the right direction, but it didn't matter; we were relieved to at least recognize somewhere. Long thin palm trees jettisoned into the sky along the sidewalks, and the architecture of the buildings had an old-time Western town vibe, and everywhere were pickup trucks of every shape, size, and color, zipping through the streets.

As we continued down the boulevard, the buildings and cars began to look more expensive, and we could see hills popping up in the distance. I found where we were on the map, and sure enough, we were coming up on Hollywood Boulevard. We were still far from the Whisky, but we were getting closer. Buildings were starting to grow taller, and billboards surrounded us. All kinds of Asian restaurants and taco stands were busy with tourists. Anthony shouted out, "Look!" while pointing out the window, where we saw the iconic red stars and black marble on the sidewalks. We passed the famous Mann's Chinese Theater. Further on, the street turned more residential and greener, first with apartments, then condos, then houses, and the houses got bigger and more ornate as the landscape rose up around us.

We came to Laurel Canyon Boulevard and turned left, and eventually were back on Sunset Blvd with the shops, gas stations, clubs, fast-food joints, and more billboards everywhere. We passed a single old-style train car sitting in a parking lot that we would learn later was Carney's hot dog and burger joint. We passed the world-famous Comedy Store and then Tower Records. We were getting close. Turning into the left lane, we slowed down, and sure enough, there in front of us was the famous Whisky a Go-Go awning, beaming like a rock and roll sunrise. Holy shit, we made it!! We pulled around into a back alley behind the building and parked. As Rick shut the engine down, we all sat still for a moment, taking in the sounds of the city outside the windows. The bus was so loud when it was moving that once it stopped and the engine was off, it was like hearing for the first time. We looked at each other, sunburned, dirty, eyes bloodshot, and collectively started laughing. I thought to myself, what the hell were we doing here? It was ridiculous. What if they don't even know who we are, and we drove all that way for nothing?

The history of the Whisky a Go-Go started when it first opened its doors in 1964. Because of city zoning laws not allowing a club to be named after an alcohol, the Whisky removed the 'e' from the name, which was leased from the French bar Whisky a Gogo located in Juan-les-Pins. The Whisky became the place where many famous bands got their start, like The Doors, Janice Joplin, Frank Zappa, Led Zeppelin, Black Sabbath, Alice Cooper, Van Halen, Mötley Crüe, and Guns and Roses, just to name a few. It had become a kind of shrine for rockers, and especially for the new glam metal scene. Our story started behind the building, parking next to the garbage dumpsters. Rick stayed with the bus, and the boys and I got out and walked back around to the front of the club. I was nervous and excited. Remembering the history of the place as I stood at the entrance made me feel like I was way out of my league and that this was a moment of truth. I walked up to the doors, pulled down the lever, and the door opened.

Upon walking inside, an odorous whiff of stale beer and cleaning products assaulted my nostrils. It was a nice-sized club, with a raised stage and a band back line, a balcony, cushioned booths, and that infamous red and black vibe. There was a dude behind the bar cleaning glasses, his long, straight black hair tucked under a blue bandanna. I walked over to him and introduced myself. "Hey brother, I'm Sully. My band, The Dirty Rain, is playing here in a couple of days, and we just drove here from New York in our bus and parked in the back of the building." He stopped what he was doing and looked at all of us up and down and said "You just arrived now?" "Yeah," I said, "and we have a bus parked out back." He said the bus would be ok for now, but if it stayed there longer than a day or two it could get towed. We asked if we could store some of our gear in the club for a couple of days before the gig. He thought it would be ok, but we would have to wait for the house tech or the manager to open the storage. But if we wanted, we could bring the gear in for now if it helped us feel more secure. He was a cool guy. The back line on the stage had speaker cabinets and drums, so we just needed our amps, guitars, cymbals, snare, and pedals, but we kept the guitars with us so we could rehearse.

We walked back to the bus and grabbed the gear. Rick parked the bus in a way that blocked the front and back doors against the wall, and we exited through the emergency exits on the roof and then climbed down off the bus. When we got everything in the club, the bartender offered us beers. We sat at a table, drank, smoked, and waited. I could tell the boys were nervous because that's usually what prompted our one-upmanship game, which usually started with a belch, a fart, a snide comment, or a flick of a cigarette and usually ended up with someone getting a drink poured over their head. It was the way we released steam or distracted ourselves from thinking about any sort of responsibility or just plain impatience. And besides, it was fucking fun. In this case, we were making fun of how awful we all looked. My hair especially was a mess, like a dread locked alley cat. Our clothes were dirty, our eyes bloodshot, and I'm pretty sure we didn't smell like roses. Hopefully, the cigarettes covered up our odor, but before our antics got physical, the manager arrived.

The bartender explained who we were, and we explained why we had arrived a few days early. Since we had no idea what to expect when we arrived and no connections in LA, we had nowhere else to go. He seemed to sympathize and let us lock our gear in storage until the gig. He also mentioned that the bus would probably be ok for a day or two but warned that the cops had been coming down hard on folks living on the streets inside their vehicles and that they were being towed away and charging big bucks to get them back, so be very careful. We were relieved that we could dock the whale for a couple of days and focus on preparing for the gig and were willing to take the chance. Right as we finished our conversation with the manager, the house engineer and the bands playing that night started trickling in for a sound check.

Each musician that came in had hair down to their ass and puffed up with gobs of hair spray. And you couldn't tell who was who in which band; they all looked like they wore the same uniform. I would learn later on that many of those hairdos were hair extensions or sometimes even wigs. They all had similar personalities, which were also very uniform like they all went to the same David Lee Roth school of bravado. That vibe is a riot when it's coming from Diamond Dave, but when it's spoken like it's being read from a script, it kind of loses its cool factor.

I couldn't relate to that kind of conformity in the name of rock and roll. Even their names were the same, like Taz or Tuff or Tango, whatever. It already seemed dated to me, not genuine or sustainable, but that is what some people think rock and roll is: cheap, easy, disposable junk food. For me, rock and roll is a spiritual thang, not a commercial enterprise or a fad, and it didn't matter if it was god or the devil to me; it was still spiritual. But for these dudes, and they were all dudes, it was about the fame, which I had nothing against, except I could hear those intentions in the music. But then I thought, who are we, or who am I, and were we really any different, or better, or am I just psyching myself out, preparing for failure?

Mitch and Anthony embraced the hair metal craze and actually related to it, and I slightly envied them for that. Why did it matter so much to me what state rock music was in, and how come I didn't flow with its inevitable progression or regression? I started writing some of these thoughts down on the cocktail napkins. We stayed for every sound check, and again, there was that uniformity. Each band had the tapping guitarist, the acrobatic shouter, the circus drummer twirling the sticks, and the static, serious, comic relief bass player chugging on eighth notes.

Damn that Van Halen, they were so good they hypnotized every hard rock guitar band after them and turned them into Van Halen clones. I remember hearing Van Halen for the first time. It was 1978, and their first single, a cover of the Kinks classic 'You Really Got Me,' came on the radio. It was the guitar tone that just grabbed me by the ears and ripped my head off.

I had no idea what they looked like, but because of the heavy tone, I imagined they looked like leather-skinned giants covered in spikes and chains with shaved heads and tattoos. Compared to other 70s hard rock at the time, their sound was more bare, more minimalistic, having more room for the heavy guitar frequencies. In a way, the mix was kind of off balance, with the guitar way up in your face. I got their debut record as soon as it came out. When I saw that they were skinny dudes with long hair and that the chicks were digging it, I knew they were going to be huge. After the sound checks we decided to walk around town a bit and come back later for the show.

We walked just down the street to another Sunset strip icon, The Rainbow Bar and Grill. Opened in 1972, the Rainbow, also known as The Rain-blow, became a hangout for famous musicians like Keith Moon, Alice Cooper, John Lennon, Ringo Starr, Elvis Presley, and Johnny Cash. As the 80s metal scene took off, the Rainbow would become the launching pad for a new wave of rockers. With its lush interior, lodge like exterior, and famous people memorabilia on the walls, we felt like we entered the coolest Hollywood theme restaurant or the cleverest of tourist traps. They served a mix of Italian American-style diner fare with a full bar. We grabbed one of the many red vinyl booths and piled ourselves in, ordering a round of drinks and a side of fries, and we came prepared with our flasks of whiskey full so as to top off our drinks when they got low. The waitresses were dressed just like the bands they loved, with their big hair sprayed and dyed and lots of cheap jewelry and eyeliner, and they were very friendly.

Our waitress looked very young. We told her about our show, and she asked for flyers to hang up, but we didn't have any. She said we had to have flyers promoting the show and hand them out to anyone and everyone. Supposedly, that's what all the bands did. And then, as if on cue, the bands we just met at the Whisky strutted in loud and proud, doing just that, handing out flyers to everyone. It started to get louder and more crowded in the restaurant as The Velvet Underground's 'Waiting for My Man' oozed out of the speakers, and I was starting to feel a little drunk. Then these three very fleshy girls came in with very little clothing on, pounds of cleavage, not particularly attractive, but extremely enthusiastic. They had way too much makeup on, and what little clothes they were wearing didn't fit very well. They also were handing out flyers, so we assumed they were a band, but no, it turned out they were fans of the bands they were promoting. I never saw anything like that in New York. This was really a scene, a community that was energized and dedicated and could probably explain the uniformity and conformity all around us. These bands weren't necessarily individual artists or innovators as much as a mob or an invading army.

In the late 60s and early 70s, bands like Black Sabbath and Judas Priest, the real grandfathers of heavy metal, came from drab apocalyptic industrial towns like Birmingham, England, and they were more like local freaks wanting to escape the environment that they wrote about in their songs, whereas these California metal heads were raised in the coastal sunshine, surrounded by a sea of bikini-clad wannabe starlets and every major record company located just blocks away. These new rockers were business and marketing-savvy, true capitalists willing to do anything to give the audience what they wanted for a chance at the brass ring. Here was the American dream in action, or nightmare, depending on which side of the fence you stood. I appreciated their work ethic, but something left a bad taste in my mouth. Perhaps I was jealous of their unabashed ambition and the power it portrayed, or maybe it was their ignorance of a fickle pop music audience. Coming from New York, I experienced people turning their backs on heavy rock for more commercial sounds. I kept writing down all these thoughts and feelings on the cocktail napkins.

Then, these three very fleshy girls made their way to our table and handed us their flyers. Since they were so very friendly, we invited them to join us. Of course, they wanted to see the bus once we told them our story. We paid the bill and headed back to the Whisky. We sent Rick ahead of us to pull the bus out so we could access the door. Back on the street, there were people everywhere, bar hopping on the strip between The Rainbow, The Whisky, The Roxy, and Gazzarri's, and most of them were wasted, long-haired metal dudes. There was a line building up in front of the Whisky. We walked around back, hopped on the bus, and opened a bottle of Jack. The girls were impressed that we had cassettes by new L.A. bands Guns and Roses, Jane's Addiction, Red Hot Chile Peppers, Fishbone, and Faster Pussycat.

I got them as promos right before I left the record store. I didn't care so much for the Faster

Pussycat but the others were played constantly. It was obvious these girls wanted more than Jack Daniels as the clothing they were barely wearing started to slowly come off, and the spanking paddles came out. We started cheering them on, and our howls and whistling caught the attention of the street as people came up to the bus. In a matter of minutes, the alley was now a party, and inside, the bus was turning into another orgy. One thing was for sure: these glam rockers were ready for sex anytime, anywhere with anyone. The bus started to get so packed Rick, and I had to stop the stampede from coming in. This went on for hours, and it was fun and all, but I was wasted and exhausted, and the only thing in my system were fries, alcohol, and cigarettes and everyone was pissing in the alley behind the bus, and it started to stank.

As the action wound down, some partiers moved to an after-party at a hotel down the street. I needed a walk to clear my head, so I tagged along with the crowd. Something about the streets and all the people made me feel lonely. I realized I wasn't keeping in touch with my family and friends back home. I don't think any of us were, and it played on my psyche. On one level, I was right where I thought I wanted to be, but on another level, I felt lost. But the truth is, I was probably just sleep-deprived. The place we arrived at was an old rundown hotel that supposedly was getting torn down, so the event was like a closing party. Once inside, I wandered into the back where there was a swimming pool that was covered, and beside it, several lounge chairs. I flopped down on the furthest one from the building.

It felt good to be vertical. The weather was perfect, with a clear black sky. I leaned back and closed my eyes while listening to the party raging as if I was listening to an album, and slowly, I slipped into a meditative state, kind of half awake, half asleep. My body was trying to communicate to me but it was in a language I couldn't quite understand. I know now it was just trying to tell me that I needed rest, good food, and some sobriety, but since that wasn't going to happen anytime soon, I just pushed those thoughts back down into my subconscious. I had no idea how much time had passed but then I began hearing a sound I instantly recognized. I opened one of my eyes, and there, about 10 feet away from me in the shadows, were a couple, that I believe were fucking. I took that as a sign it was time to stand up. When I did, I actually felt much better and I walked back into the party. The Ramones were blasting out of a large boombox in one of the rooms.

There were open vodka bottles and plastic cups. I helped myself and walked around the rundown hotel. There were people snorting coke off of TVs and kitchen counters, and in one room, they were snorting it off an overturned acoustic guitar that was being passed around. Some of the people at the party looked like they were street vagrants or homeless, while others looked like models and movie stars, and they were all partying together. The vibe was different than New York. I couldn't comprehend it then, but looking back, it was way more Caucasian physically, with more blonds and blue eyes, and more American culturally, with conversations revolving around who was signed to a major label or had a manager or who got a new car or house. I don't know how else to describe it, but there was a sense of desperation in the air.

Once that guitar was licked clean, it was left on one of the hotel beds, so I bravely picked it up. It was slightly fucked up, but I was able to get it somewhat in tune. I started to play some delta blues riffs that caught the attention of some of the partygoers, and people started listening. Then one rocker dude who was very wasted began to sing along with what I was playing, doing his best Steven Tyler impression, and he wasn't even that bad, improvising lyrics on the spot about his girlfriend kicking him out of the house because he was high. Other people began to bang out beats on the walls, and it kind of turned into a drunken open-mic karaoke jam with different people making up their own songs, some being surprisingly hilarious. One girl sang about the methadone clinic turning her away.

After a while, I handed the guitar to someone else, but they didn't last long with it, and then the party began to wind down. Besides the jamming and making up songs, I didn't really connect with anyone, but then again, my head wasn't in a great place, and I'm pretty sure I wasn't looking so good. Heading back to the bus, I was hoping to find some food, but everything was closed. The walk back was lonely but beautiful, and the temperature was just right. There were still people hanging around the bus when I got there, and Anthony, Shane, and Rick were chilling inside, but there was no sign of Mitch. I learned that he left with one of the random girls that hopped onto the bus. Good for him. He will have a bed and a shower and probably some food, not to mention the sex. I searched the bus for food and dug out an unopened box of Cheerios, plopped down on the couch, opened it up, and ate out of the box with my hands. Inside was a coupon for a free Egg McMuffin. I stuck that in my pocket. Then I found a jar of peanut butter and stuck my finger into the brown paste using it as a spoon. Welcome to Los Angeles.

THE BUS

Besides being woken a few times during the night by sounds outside the bus, I slept better than I had in a while, but in the morning, I desperately needed a bathroom, water, and some decent food. The Boys were still half asleep, and since Mitch had yet to return, we couldn't move the bus anyway, so I figured I might as well venture out on my own. I walked to The Rainbow, which technically wasn't open yet, but I begged a cleaning person inside to let me use the bathroom, and amazingly, he did. Looking into the bathroom mirror, I didn't look so great. I wiped most of my body down with paper towels and hand soap, and that was definitely an improvement. I thanked the cleaning person as I left and I did feel a little better. I continued to walk on Sunset Boulevard, looking for food. After a while, I came upon a salon called New York Hair and looked at my reflection in the window. The dreads were getting worse. I took it as a sign. I made a mental note of going back there and cutting them out. A little further down the road was a small delicatessen.

I walked in and looked around. They had hero sandwiches but called them subs. I ordered an extra-long sausage egg and cheese and told them to cut it in quarters and also a bottle of water and a big bag of chips. I brought the food back to the bus, and that inspired the boys to get up. While we were shoveling food in our faces, we heard a car pull up next to the bus. It was Mitch getting out of a cab. He jumped on the bus and collapsed on the couch, giggling like a kid. "Everything ok?" I asked. "It was way better last night than it was this morning." he chuckled. "What happened?" I pried. "I sobered up!" he laughed. I had to hand it to Mitch when it came to sex; he was a true Democrat. He also brought with him a local rocker magazine that had information on every band, stage, club, bar, record store, music store, and cool clothing shop in Southern California. There were also rehearsal and recording studios listed.

I thought out loud, "Hey, maybe we should rehearse." Everyone agreed. After finding the addresses on our map, I marked the closest ones on the paper, grabbed some change and walked to the pay phone I noticed on my walk earlier in the morning. On the phone, I got a rehearsal room booking at the first place I called, and supposedly there was parking for the bus. We still had some time before the rehearsal, so I headed to the New York hair salon that I had also passed earlier. As I walked inside, there was a beautiful stylish Asian woman sitting at the reception desk with a glowing smile. I asked if they accepted walk-ins. She asked what I wanted done. I wanted the back cut short, but the front left long. That would get rid of the dreads but also add some edge. She said sure and took me to the back of the shop to wash my hair. "Man," I thought. "I'm going to cut my hair." I knew it was going to be an issue with the boys, but that didn't really bother me. My issue was going from very long hair to short hair. Doing that has always had a very strong mental and physical effect on me. My hair was very long, and it had been a long time since I last had it cut, but it needed to be done. After having my hair washed, she sat me in the chair and started cutting right into the dreads in the back of my head. Big chunks of hair fell to the floor. Oh boy,

I thought, no turning back now. Little by little, my whole look had been drastically transformed.

When I arrived back at the bus, I got every reaction possible. Mitch was shaking his head in disgust, Anthony looked on in shock, Shane was laughing, and Rick just had one eyebrow raised. I had to admit, I felt a little naked. "Come, you freak," blurted Shane, "We're gonna be late." We fired up the bus and headed to the rehearsal studio that was located in an office complex across town. It was confusing trying to find the place because it was obscured by an apartment building and set back off the street, so we kept missing it, but Rick noticed some dudes loading a van with amps and drums, and that turned out to be the place. We were able to park right in front. The bus needed to get organized. We had drugs, paraphernalia, and money stashed in every nook and cranny, spread out in several bags and cases.

My personal bag was trashed, and my clothes were all over the place. I stuffed everything I could find into that bag and took it in with me to take inventory of what was still possible to wear.

Everyone else did the same. So, with our bags, guitars, and sticks, we headed inside. The reception area was pretty raw, with rows of shelves loaded up with drums and cymbals. There were hundreds of cables hanging from the wall. Plus, a soda and a cigarette machine. Some tattooed biker-looking dudes were behind the desk. I told them who we were, and they pointed to a door down the hall.

We walked through it into a decent-sized room with a slightly raised stage riser, a full back line, PA, tables, couches, and stage lighting. It was much bigger and much better equipped than anything in New York at the same price range. Our guitars had definitely taken a beating from the extreme temperatures of the desert and we needed to change the strings, which we did first so at least they would be stretched out by show time. We lost a half hour doing that, and once we started to play, we struggled to stay in tune, and unfortunately, the heads on the studio drums were beaten to shit, and the cymbals were cracked.

Luckily the amps and the PA were pretty good and loud, so we cranked it, warming up with a little T-Rex Bang a Gong. There was definitely some rust flying around, but slowly, we eventually loosened up. Finally, we dialed in the PA, the amps, and the tuning and hit a groove. After running through the sets a few times, we took a break, and I tried folding some clothes while the boys laid out the assortment of powders, pills, and ganja that we still had left. We were running low. They also handed me some cash because we've been leaning hard on my credit card. I picked out what I would wear for the show and separated my dirty clothes from the few clean things I had left. After a few bumps of blow, a few shots, and a few puffs, we started feeling good, but it was still early in the afternoon. We called it rock and roll brunch. We played through the sets a few more times and then had seconds and then thirds of our rock and roll brunch. Once we got started on a binge, it was hard to stop us. We ended up funking up the room because cigarette ash caught fire to the rug, but it felt good to play, and it definitely lifted our spirits, even though I could tell Mitch was still pissed about my haircut.

THE BUS

We were so lucky Rick was with us because he stayed sober to drive and help move the gear because, of course, we were trashed again. We played right through our scheduled time, and one of the Biker-looking dudes had to come in to tell us our time was up.

After the rehearsal, we headed back to The Whisky and parked the bus in the same spot. Mitch, Shane, and I walked into the club with our guitars to see if we could also lock them up in the club's storage till the next night's gig which they allowed us to. We were definitely paranoid about theft, and doing that put us at ease. After shimmying the bus against the walls to block the doors, we strolled back over to the Rainbow to hang out. That place was like a centrifugal force for every wannabe rock star and every real rockstar in Hollywood, and this time, we spread ourselves around and made casual conversations with anybody who was open to it. I spoke with this one kid who was so hyper he was either on something or had a mental health issue, but he was very entertaining. He complained about how fake the scene was, that all these bands were the same, and that the real deal was in England.

He would literally call rocker dudes who walked by him posers, and they would totally ignore him. I also met this woman who looked like a Rockabilly Elvira with massive cleavage and black lipstick. She also seemed a little disturbed in the head, but we talked about Alister Crowley and the California Church of Satan. I spoke with a Vietnam War veteran who had a cane and long gray hair in a ponytail and said he came to California in the '70s from the East Coast and never went back. After a while, the night became a blur. I was drunk, my band was drunk, the whole Rainbow was blasted, and that was the charm of the place. It was considered normal behavior, so everyone stayed relaxed and chill. That being said, there were a few moments when some folks were escorted out, but it was just another day at the office for the people working there. You felt you were in good hands. I do remember walking around and checking out some other clubs like The Roxy and Gazzari's, but eventually, we were back on the bus with some random rockers from The Whisky, and we partied again into the night.

I didn't remember when I fell asleep but waking up was not easy. I fell asleep sitting up with my head leaning on the window which made my whole body hurt, but especially the side of my face. It was already noon, and everyone was still sleeping; I couldn't believe it was the day of the show, and I felt like shit. All I could smell were alcohol and cigarettes, and I couldn't tell if it was me or the bus. I had to get some air. The sky was bright blue, and the sun was shining, but inside, I felt the complete opposite, like a vampire left in the sun to die. I walked for a while on Sunset Boulevard as if I was searching for someone or something. It was like I had to keep moving, or I was going to snap. I encountered all types of people on my walk. Drunks, punks, junkies, muscle dudes, street performers, yuppies, tourists, vendors, I struck up a conversation with all of them to perhaps distract myself from the way I felt, and it kind of worked, so I circled back towards the bus. When I got back Shane and Rick were hanging out drinking beer.

Anthony and Mitch were at the Rainbow. Shane handed me a beer, but I passed. We sat and chatted for a while. It was obvious that Anthony and Mitch were very attracted to the Hollywood scene that we've experienced so far. We talked about the offer in Austin and what should be our next plan. One reality we had to face is that Rick would have to get back to New York pretty soon and that could be a potential problem if we decided to stay on the road. Another obvious issue was money which was slowly dwindling down. With no real answers or conclusions, we closed up the bus and headed over to The Rainbow to hang out before our sound check at The Whisky. It was a highlight of the trip when we passed the front of the Whisky to see our band name being added to the marquee. We had no disposable cameras left so we decided to look for a store to buy one. Luckily, we were in a tourist part of town, so it wasn't too difficult to find them. Afterward, we went to the Rainbow and grabbed Mitch and Anthony to take some pictures. For the first couple of shots, we just stood there, but after a while, we began our usual antics of pushing each other's buttons to the point where some people walking by thought it was a gang fight, and Rick had to assure them, we were just fucking around. The crew from the Whisky started arriving and let us get our stuff and set up early since we were already there.

They had a great stage with full monitors and professional lighting and microphones that didn't look like they were in a war. The equivalent to The Whisky in New York would have been the historic CBGBs, which had a terrible stage, blown monitors, and microphones so dented and covered in body fluids they'd be condemned by the Board of Health. Our soundcheck went well, except for the soundman not appreciating Anthony not having a mic hole cut out of his kick drum head. We had plenty of time to dial everything in, but the reality was there would be a band that would play before us, so unfortunately, in that kind of situation, all the work we did for sound check could all be in vain, but hey, that's rock and roll. We practiced until the other bands started coming in, and then we got off the stage to let them sound check. I stuck around to check out the other bands, which were both very similar to the bands we saw the other night. There was definitely a pattern going on, and it was very strange for us to have the night start so early.

In New York, it wasn't uncommon for shows to start at midnight or even later, but by 8 o'clock, the Hollywood crowd started rolling in, and I was feeling nervous. They had beers for us in the dressing room, and we mostly hung out back there, smoking and chatting with some of the other bands and their friends. Eventually, the first band went on, and we watched from upstairs. They were like bubblegum metal, and it sounded like the board operator was struggling to get the vocalist in the mix. There weren't that many people in the audience, and only their girlfriends really shouted and applauded, but again, they at least had a lot of energy. Their songs were short, and so was their set, but they took forever to get off the stage.

THE BUS

Finally, we were able to get on, but Anthony had to rearrange the drum kit radically, so it still took some time before we started. Lucky for us, a few more people came into the club, so at least there would be an audience to hear us. Looking back now, I realize as a band, we never took the time to connect with each other before this seminal moment and acknowledge what we had pulled off to get there, and I think that may have been a missed opportunity.

Anthony gave a thumbs up, so I signaled the sound guy. I stepped up to the mic and announced, "We're The Dirty Rain, and we just drove across the country to play this place; thank you for having us," and Anthony counted us off. From the first note we all noticed the sound was nothing like our sound check. My guess is the sound guy got the order of the mixes wrong. I know that I had difficulties connecting with the band, the audience, and myself. We struggled to find the pocket. At the end of each song, the audience reaction was polite but I got the feeling we weren't changing anybody's life. We carried on with the set, playing it cool, letting our music and attitude just be, and fifty minutes later, just like that, it was over. Talk about anti-climactic. We grabbed our gear and numbly left the stage. I felt empty. Thankfully the Whisky lets us lock up our gear again, and we got right down to the business of heading to the bar and getting fucked up.

A few people did come up to us mentioning that they dug our sound and wanted to know who we were. Then, this gorgeous Mexican goth girl named Anna introduced herself to me, and we got touchy-feely at the bar very quickly, so I brought her upstairs to the dressing room. Since the last band was on stage and my band and the first band were at the bar, we had the dressing room to ourselves, and touchy-feely quickly became Californication. It was also the first time I was with someone who had a pierced tongue, and she definitely put it to good use. At some point, I believe the door opened because the music from the stage suddenly got louder, then lower again, but we didn't stop. But when the door opened and closed again, I figured this would be a good time to introduce my new friend to the bus.

THE BUS

As Anna and I stepped out of the club, I felt so grateful to have her close to me because I was feeling depressed about our subpar show, and she definitely took my mind off of that. I couldn't wait to surprise her and be naked with her on the bus, but as we turned the corner, my worst nightmare happened right before my eyes. A huge tow truck was pulling our bus out of its hiding space at the back of the Whisky. I screamed my lungs out, "WAIT!" and ran and jumped up onto the tow truck's big round circular wheel wells.

Two police cars with their lights flashing were blocking the street, and when the cops sitting inside saw me jumping onto the tow truck, they quickly got out and pulled me down off of the trailer. As I was getting handled by the cops, I turned to Anna and shouted, "Please, go get my band"! and she ran back inside on a mission. The cops threw me against their car and pinned me down. "It's my bus"! I cried. They eventually let me loose but demanded ID. Shane, Rick, Anthony, and a few other people came flying out of the bar. Not Mitch because, as I would later learn, he already had left with the same girl from the night before. Everyone was shouting at the police and I could see from the corner of my eye one cop getting on the radio.

Another cop shouted back at us, "This vehicle is going to be towed, and if anyone interferes, they will be arrested." I literally fell to my knees and begged, "Please don't do this." but it didn't matter; the cops stood their ground. Shane calmly pleaded if we could at least get some personal items off the bus but they did not compromise. Another cop wrote something out on a piece of paper and handed it to me along with my license. Then he said in a cold, robotic voice, "Call this number tomorrow to find where your vehicle has been taken, then pay the fines, and you'll get your vehicle back." By this time, some of the folks from the club came out and tried to reconcile the situation, but it was too late, the bus was leaving. We were fucked.

Luckily, we still had most of our personal items, contraband, and our instruments and amps at the club, and the people there felt terrible about our situation and offered to house us, at least individually, for the night. But instead of separating, we decided to stick together. The crazy thing was, because there were no cell phones yet, we had no idea where Mitch was and no way to get in touch with him, but we were pretty sure he was in a much better situation then we were. I was so distracted by this disaster I forgot all about Anna, who seemed to have disappeared, and the club was starting to close for the night, but they were very gracious, letting us continue storing our stuff. But that wasn't an open invitation. They gave us a week. In all fairness, we were warned that the bus could be towed away. We dropped the ball and were about to learn the hard way what that would mean.

What the hell were we going to do? I told the boys about the party at the condemned hotel that I stumbled into our first night, and since it wasn't too far, we decided to walk over there. On the walk over, a black cloud feeling came over me. I may have been in shock. I was so pissed off at myself that I started having thoughts like, maybe this was a sign, and I should jump on a plane and just go back to New York, but I didn't say any of this out loud. The hotel was closed, and there was a security guard sitting in a car in the parking lot. We walked across the street to a bus stop bench just to sit and think. We were exhausted. And then the strangest thing happened. Two skinny dudes with long hair walking swiftly in the street were singing in what sounded like some strange yodel language. It wasn't till after they passed us that I realized it was Lars Ulrich and Jason Newstead of Metallica! After the initial shock, I shouted out, "METALLICA!" They were already up the street, and then they jumped into a car and took off. I didn't know what to think. It was bizarre and, in a way, made me even more depressed.

These two humans at the top of their game just strolled by us, sitting at the bottom of ours. That was brutal. It was the middle of the night, and everything was closed. We saw one cab, and it flew right by us. There was nothing else to do but to start walking. We were in a tourist part of the city so we knew eventually we would find a hotel. The first one we came upon had a no vacancy sign, so we kept walking. The second one also had a no vacancy sign, but this time, we went in to see if they could help us find a place. We walked into an empty lobby, and there was no one at the check-in counter. There was a big button on the front desk with a sign that said press after hours, so I did. We didn't hear anything but decided to wait anyway. They had some chairs in the lobby, so we took a load off and sat down. Still, no one came, so I kept riding that buzzer. Eventually, an old guy who looked like he just rolled out of bed came out and, in a thick Spanish accent, asked what we wanted.

Once he realized we weren't guests, he curtly asked us to leave. We explained we just needed our bearings and asked him to please point us to the next closest hotel, which he obliged by waving in the direction we had been heading in, and then he disappeared from where he came. As we got back out on the street, another cab passed us by and didn't stop. I didn't blame them; four freaks walking in the street in the middle of the night probably wasn't worth the risk. We walked for a while before we saw a hotel sign up ahead of us. Before walking in I proposed that it might be better if I go in alone. This was a much fancier place and a bit livelier inside. There were people in the lobby and someone at the front desk. I found out they only had one room available, a double, with an eleven o'clock check out, and it was very expensive. I asked if they could extend the check-out till noon or one, but they said the room was already booked, so no. I handed over my credit card and ID.

Back in the 80's credit cards weren't digitized yet. They usually were just pushed through a carbon copy machine or called in over the phone, the latter being the policy of this hotel. I waited as the checkout person made the call and recited my card numbers into the phone. "I'm sorry, sir, but your card was declined," was their response. "What, wait, why?" I choked. "Insufficient funds" was the reply. "Can you try again?" My card and ID were handed back to me. I walked back outside to the boys. "Do you think you maxed out the card?" asked Shane. "I guess it's possible," I confessed. I had dropped the ball with keeping track of the finances so I wasn't sure. We sat our asses down on another set of benches and counted the money we had on us. It wasn't much. It would only be a couple of hours till the sun would start to come up. We just needed to keep it together till we found out where the bus went. We were tired of walking, so we just zoned out on the benches.

This was definitely a low point of the trip, and I was just waiting for the cops to come by and bust us for vagrancy or something even worse. It felt like an eternity sitting there as Anthony and Rick actually fell asleep while Shane and I talked and talked. We discussed how we both felt like we didn't fit into the New York music business scene, that we were just as alienated here in LA, and that perhaps Austin was the best way to go. Slowly, the sun came up, and Hollywood began to awake. Damn, we just spent the night living on the street in LA. Luckily, the weather was on our side, not hot or cold or raining. We just needed to get our shit together, and I needed to take a shit.

It's amazing how people today will never experience a phone booth, but back in the day, humans would enter a standalone structure on the sidewalk made of glass and steel with a folding door that, when closed, would block out the external sound so you could put metal coins into a slot, punch in or dial a phone number, and basically have a private conversation. Even crazier is sometimes there would be an actual physical phonebook inside the booth, or better yet, you could dial zero and get an actual human called an operator, to find and connect you to a number. Hundreds, thousands, or perhaps even millions of people could have used the same phone booth that I was standing in. I dialed the number the cop gave me and was told there were several locations the bus could have been brought too.

They said it could take a day or two or more before the bus was logged in and processed, so we would have to keep calling till we tracked it down.

Well, it was official: we were homeless. Since there was nothing more we could do about the bus, we each took turns calling people back in New York to check in and to see if anyone had any connections or resources we could use. Turns out a friend of Anthony's knew someone who moved to L.A. a couple of years earlier and gave us their number. He dialed it, but there was no answer. Defeated, the only thing we could do was crawl back to the Rainbow, hoping to reconnect with Mitch and to pray for a miracle.

The walk back to the Rainbow was rough. We were exhausted, dirty, embarrassed, low on money, and worried. The place wasn't even open yet, so we hung outside for a while. One of the waitresses we met a couple of days before had arrived, and she let us in and served us coffee. She mentioned she heard about what happened with the bus and felt bad and that if we needed anything to please let her know. The folks at the Rainbow were very cool. We sat there for hours, drinking coffee. I practically took a whole shower in their bathroom sink. When I returned to the table, Anthony had gone back to the phone booth to make some more calls while I was taking a paper towel bath, and he had finally gotten through to the contact his friend in New York had given him earlier. His name was Chris, and he relayed that he was on his way out of town but would meet us at the rainbow in a couple of days. Not the best news we could have heard but at least it was something. Then, as if right on schedule, Mitch walked in with a confused look on his face, probably because we must have looked so ecstatic to see him, and he probably wondered where the hell the bus was. He sat there in amazement as we told him what we'd just been through. I didn't realize it then but looking back at it now, that was the first break in the band.

I could see it in Mitch's whole demeanor and body language. He was abandoning the ship, whether he was conscious of it or not. Rick, too was floating the idea that maybe if he flew back earlier, he could be more of a help back in New York and less of a hanger on here. Did they think we weren't going to get the bus back? It was depressing, and I needed to clear my head. I asked the waitress if there were any places just to chill nearby, and she said there was a park within walking distance. I was exhausted and couldn't relax at the Rainbow, so I decided I'd walk to the park. Anthony and Shane came along, but Mitch and Rick hung back. After making a wrong turn and forgetting the name of the park, I just asked someone on the street if there was a park nearby and they pointed us in a direction. What we found wasn't much of a park, but there was grass and trees, and we could at least sit in the shade as all three of us fell down onto the dusty grass and stretched out. I felt the coffee running through my veins as I slipped in and out of a shallow sleep, plagued with maddening dreams filled with demon-like antagonists inside a labyrinth of vortexes. Time drifted away, and my strained, aching body slipped into darkness.

I was startled awake by the sound of a dog barking, and I had no idea where I was or how long I was out for. Anthony and Shane both looked peacefully asleep. The cool, dusky feeling of the ground got inside my bones, and the dry air coated my skin. I sat up and rubbed my eyes. Everything looked different for reasons I couldn't explain, almost as if I was seeing in a new way. I was hungry, not just for food and drink, but for meaning, purpose, and adventure. I woke the boys, and we headed back to the Rainbow. We found Rick at the bar in a deep conversation with some old dude looking like Bela Lugosi, and Mitch was nowhere in sight. Turns out Mitch split with the girl he's been staying with but left her phone number and address with Rick, written on a rolled-up dollar bill inside a baggie with half an eight-ball of coke. Rick also bought a pint of vodka that he had hidden under his shirt. We grabbed a booth and ordered some French fries with a round of iced water and lemon that we spiked with vodka. We passed around the baggie and Anthony's coke spoon, doing multiple bumps. Mitch mentioned to Rick that the girl's place he was crashing at wouldn't be able to host all of us but maybe one or two. "Or we could sniff this whole bag and drink this whole bottle and stay out all night," quipped Shane, and to that, we raised our glasses.

THE BUS

As it turned out, the experience we were having was just another typical night at the Rainbow, with every Hollywood freak, out-of-work actor, wanna-be rock star, and tourist, sitting at life's crossroads alongside random famous people. We were giving the staff bumps of blow and they would return the favor with food and drink. Total strangers who had heard about the impounded bus were buying us drinks. It was bizarre. One dude told us where the bus was probably towed to, but it could take days until it's in the system to know for sure. The real bad news is it could cost a shit ton of money to get it out, and that just caused us more depression and hence more drinking. Our little booth party grew as we had a few very nice girls join in, and they seemed to really want to take care of us. We stayed at the Rainbow practically the whole day. The girls were heading to another party and invited us. We had nowhere else to be, so we went along, stuffed inside their green Dodge Dart. We ended up in some dark, smokey loft hidden in a downtown back alley. There was a DJ, a makeshift bar, and Christmas lights hanging from the ceiling.

The crowd was more punk goth than hard rock metal but super chill, and everyone was just drinking and talking and, once in a while, dancing to a Depeche Mode song. We collapsed on some old couches they had in the back. I felt really drunk, but the coke was keeping me steady; but also hurting my jaw from unconsciously grinding my teeth. I usually don't do well with stimulants because I'm naturally hyperactive, but at the moment, I appreciated the boost. It was much needed in our current situation. One of the girls we were with was the sister of the bartender and she hooked us up with a bottle of vodka that we all chipped in for at a very reduced price. I didn't remember much after that. Total blackout.

I awoke on the couch to the sound of clanging bottles, not knowing where I was for the second time in 24 hours. My head hurt, and my mouth was dry as chalk. The clanking sounds also woke up the boys, who were spread out all around me on chairs and sofas. We were the only ones still in the loft beside the person throwing out the garbage, who didn't seem concerned at all that four dudes were sleeping on the furniture. I desperately needed a toothbrush. We slowly made our way out of the loft while shielding our eyes from the outside light. It was almost noon, and the sun was coming down directly into the alleyway. We looked like the Walking Dead. The girls and their car were long gone. All we knew was we were downtown; other than that, we were lost. We made our way out of the alley and walked up the street. Somehow, walking through the downtown streets reminded me of New York and I actually felt a little better.

We walked around for a while and came upon a travel agency. Rick wanted to go inside and inquire about changing his flight back home, so in we went. When he sat with an agent, we leafed through the plethora of brochures available all around the office. I picked up one about Venice Beach and held it up for Anthony and Shane to see. They shook their heads yes and gave the thumbs up. Turned out Rick was able to move his flight, and he would be leaving us in 24 hours. That was a dose of harsh reality. There was no way we would have made it as far as we did without him. Defeated, we decided to go to the beach. The travel agent gave us a bus map, and I held onto the Venice Beach brochure.

I passed out on that packed and pungent city bus that arrived at Venice Beach almost an hour after we had left the travel agency. The sky was electric blue, the air cool and breezy as we stepped off the stuffy bus onto a crumbling street where there were pockets of homeless people living in battered tents and cardboard boxes. We were just a couple of blocks from the beach, and it felt good to walk after the long bus ride. We made our way onto the famous Venice beach boardwalk with joggers, skate punks, rollerbladers, dog walkers, and tanned bodies in shorts and bikinis, and we looked like a gang of apocalypse survivors. Everything seemed so nice and chill, but I felt a million miles away from what was right in front of me. My mind was reeling with thoughts about the bus, the band, what to do next, and where my life was going. We just strolled aimlessly on the boardwalk directionless, just taking it all in. After walking around Venice for hours, we dragged our weary bodies onto the beach towards the waves and the setting sun and collapsed there on the cooling sand. It felt good. This was it, the end of the highway, from coast to coast. Here we were, without our blue chariot, without our instruments, without our clothes even. But we were here. Now what?

We fell asleep in the sun on that beach and awoke to the night, with the bright lights from the city scorching the night sky. Peeling our sunbaked bodies off the sand we brushed each other off then headed towards the bars on the boardwalk. We were wrecked and starving. A hypnotizing aroma emanated from a crazy cheap taco stand that pulled us in like a magnet. We ordered a bunch of Chorizo, Bistecca, and El Pastors, then sat quietly on the grass, devouring each tortilla-wrapped deliciousness. Having a hot meal made me feel much better. After we ate, we debated whether we should hang out the night in Venice or head back to Hollywood. Just then, a fight broke out about fifty feet from us, so we took that as a sign.

Also, it was an uneasy feeling knowing our gear was stored in the Whisky as it was widely known about our precarious situation. Best for us to stay close by, but that would also mean maybe some of us would be sleeping on benches again. We found another payphone and dialed the number Mitch gave us. A female voice cracked through the phone speaker from an answering machine and told us to leave a message. "Yo Mitch, we will be back at the Whisky in a couple of hours, and it would be great if we could meet up," yelped Anthony into the phone. We then found a bus stop and hunkered down for the long haul.

Arriving back into the circus of Hollywood Boulevard, we lumbered towards the Whisky, which, when we got there, was rockin' as usual. It was the last place I wanted to be. I wanted so much to be back on the bus, rolling along in freedom, down a long-lost highway to somewhere unknown, but now our lives were inside of that club and it was a vulnerable state to be in. We hung around outside for a while, checking out the girls and dudes prancing around like peacocks, handing out flyers for upcoming gigs. I ended up meeting a dude who saw our show, and we got into a great conversation about the scene in Hollywood and how it was really a culture based on being famous and that the music wasn't as important. It was at that moment Mitch showed up with a few people in tow. He seemed happy.

The people he was with went inside the club, and the five of us regrouped. We swung round back to where the bus was towed from and got Mitch caught up. It was decided that Rick would get his things and go back with Mitch to the girl's place and crash the night there, then head to the airport in the morning. It was a tense moment. It felt like we were losing a limb. Something about this trip brought the five of us into a sort of unified field of being. I believe that's what traveling and playing music together does to human beings. It's like our molecular energies vibrated in harmony, and with someone leaving, it would change the tuning, and it definitely did. To celebrate Rick's completion of the journey, the first round was on him, and we headed inside the Whisky with its din of hair bands. We stayed till closing and then hung outside till the sun came up. Rick never went back with Mitch to the girl's house. I was practically delirious from a combination of cigarettes, alcohol, and sleep deprivation. Eventually, we collapsed on some benches, and I passed out. The next thing I knew, someone was shaking me. "Come on," poked Shane. "We're gonna take Rick to the airport."

JUMPING SHIP

Time seemed to distort after Rick left. I forgot what month it was, and there were more days of staying out all night, crashing on random couches, hooking up with girls, or napping in some park because we were actually homeless. What a great little system the L.A. police had for creating potential criminals, as our story moves on to Act 2. We met so many people in so many places in such a short amount of time that everything became a blur. Feeling like I had no control over anything, I sort of let go and relinquished my life and soul to the universe. We did finally meet up with Chris, the guy originally from New York that Anthony had called. He met us in the middle of the day in a graffitied-covered cargo van. A short dude wearing yellow sweatpants and brown cowboy boots. His long dyed black hair matched his chipped black nail polish and stuck out from underneath a tattered straw cowboy hat, with its rim bent way down in front of his face. We awkwardly introduced ourselves and expressed just how desperate and grateful we were for him to meet with us. He said our troubles were over and that we should come with him, so we piled into the dirty van with Anthony sitting shotgun and the rest of us sitting on the floor in the back. We drove to The Whisky to grab some of our stuff.

The staff there were relieved that we were ok and that we connected with someone who could help us, and also that we were picking up some of our stuff. They were bummed we hadn't gotten the bus back yet, but they had good news for us. A band cancelled on them, and they asked if we could fill in. I nearly cried when they asked us, and of course, we said yes. It would be in less than a week, so we left the drums and amps behind. Our next destination was a holding center for towed vehicles. Unfortunately, upon arriving, we learned the bus wasn't there. At least the cops were able to tell us that it wasn't even in their system yet. Un-fucking believable. After the impound, Chris needed to make a stop. We ended up driving up into the hills, passing luxurious houses and people walking their dogs until we pulled into a gated driveway in front of an Italian-style villa that uncharacteristically had Funkadelic's Maggot Brain crying through an open second-story window.

We all crumbled out of the van, walked to the front door and rang the doorbell. A geeky, skinny pale dude looking like he was in his forties answered the door wearing slippers and what looked like shiny blue silk pajamas. His eyes were blood red and contrasted with his glaring white dentures peeking through a crooked smile. "Christopher, my boy, you've brought friends," he announced and then waved us all inside. It seemed like we entered the aftermath of a raging party. There were empty bottles, cans, empty glasses and plates littered everywhere around the art deco-decorated bachelor pad. A giant TV was on with the sound turned down, showing stock market prices, while the Funkadelic was still bumping from upstairs. "Come in, gentleman, and take a load off", said our host, leading us to a huge sofa in the living room. We could see the pool in the back through the sliding glass doors, where three young women in bikinis and sunglasses were lying pool side. Our host pulled a wad of cash out of his pajama pocket and handed it to Chris.

Chris, in turn, handed him a rolled-up plastic baggie filled with crystal powder, which our host opened and emptied out onto a large coffee table in front of the giant sofa. He then crushed up the crystals with a large glass ashtray that was on the table. I guessed it was coke. I asked about the Funkadelic coming from upstairs, and he pleaded for me to go and put on whatever I wanted and that his vinyl collection filled an entire bedroom. I left the inevitable snorting marathon that was about to go down and pushed myself up the steep staircase. I followed the sound to a minimally furnished bedroom filled with crates of records. He had two turntables plugged into a DJ style mixer and a great collection of funk, soul, and R&B. He also had a brand-new copy of Prince's latest album 'Lovesexy.' I went straight for that. Sliding the spotless disc record out of the sleeve, I placed it on the adjacent player, cross-faded into the opening track, then laid back onto the bed in the room and let my soul slip inside the psychedelic frequency vortex of Prince's brilliant recordings.

As always, the record was a totally different sound from the prior one before it, but still undoubtedly Prince. The lyrics expressed light and dark themes about spirituality and sensuality as only Prince could. When side one was finished, I flipped the record over, and by the end of the album, it was my favorite Prince album. I followed Prince with Cameo's Word Up and headed back downstairs. The three bikini-clad girls were now inside, kneeling at the coffee table, inhaling the mounds of white powder. Between the headache, the rawness of my nostrils, the tightness in my lungs, and the nausea in my stomach, I was in no mood to drink, smoke, or snort anything, and I had the feeling the boys felt the same as me.

What we needed was a bath and some sleep. Chris was gracious enough to get us the hell out of there, and on the way to his place, he revealed to us the obvious: that he was a drug dealer. He figured we should know because we were now in the proximity of a large quantity of illegal substances. I was shocked that he trusted us with that information, but as we would eventually learn, he was pretty much a straight-up guy. His connection fronted him the stuff, and he would drive around L.A. distributing it. He was so busy that he was hoping we could help him out. We would get paid and have a place to crash and get invited to a lot of parties. It was definitely food for thought, but without any real food we weren't in our right minds to make decisions of any kind.

Shane, Anthony, and I had been crashing for a few days at Chris' place when he told us that he knew of a good deal on an apartment we could rent. We figured it would be best to take a look at it. Mitch was still hanging with the girl from the club, but three of us crashing at Chris' place was getting old fast. The rental was located on Hollywood Blvd, right across from the famous Mann's Chinese theater. It was a small studio apartment above an all-night liquor store, and you could actually see the famous Hollywood sign up in the hills from the window. We all went together in the van that afternoon. An old Latino guy let us into a two-story walk-up with only one bed, an old loveseat, and one small desk for furniture. The place had industrial grey carpeting that looked pretty new but had a nasty stain in one of the corners of the room.

We wouldn't have to put any money down, and we could move in right away. The details would be worked out later between us. We saw Chris put something in the old guy's hand, so it was pretty obvious what was going on. It was way better than being on the streets, and the location was convenient enough. He handed us the keys, and voila! Home sweet home. Chris mentioned a friend of his who lived down the hall from our room and went to see if he was home while we brought in our luggage and guitars. A few minutes later, he was back, introducing us to his friend Remi, another long-haired rocker in a too-tight t-shirt and torn jeans. We all shook hands. "From time to time, Remi may ask one or more of you to take a ride with him, cool?" Said Chris, emphasizing "cool?" by raising his eyebrows as he said it. We collectively agreed.

"The best part about this place is the liquor store downstairs stays open pretty late" he mumbled as he exited the apartment and then added. "Chill out tonight; I'll come by around two tomorrow." and then he left. Remi lingered in the doorway for a moment and then said nonchalantly, "Anyone wanna do a bump?" There was a slight pause, and then we all said yeah, sure, cool, and he gestured for us to follow him back to his place, and we walked down a dreary hallway. His place was definitely lived in.

There was shit everywhere, records, cassettes, clothes, empty bottles of soda and beer. On top of a filthy coffee table were bags of assorted powders, pills, and lots of cannabis. He poured some coke onto a mini mirror and chopped and separated it into short lines with a razor blade. He picked up a small, thin brass tube along with the mirror, stretched out his arms and with a devilish grin said, "Who's first?" and each of us partook. We parlayed some cash together, and Shane headed to the liquor store downstairs to grab something cheap and plentiful, which usually meant gin or vodka and thus began another long night of partying, which again turned into hours, then days and then weeks and then into a blur of blackouts, pass outs, and knockouts. We did eventually find out where the bus was taken and we even went down to where it was in the middle of the night.

We trailed along the huge fence that surrounded the lot till we saw our beautiful, sad, lonely bus parked practically up against the fence. On our side was a camper that practically matched the fence in height. I thought if I could climb on top of that camper, I could

THE BUS

jump over the fence and land on top of the bus. The only problem was we didn't know if anyone was inside the camper. We tried to peer through the windows, but it was too dark inside. If we knocked on the door in the middle of the night, we might have gotten shot. I took the chance and climbed up the ladder on the back end of the camper as fast as I could, got on the roof, took a running jump over the fence and landed on the roof of the bus. I opened the roof port that was never locked and lowered myself into the bus. It was pretty funky smelling. I found the camping light and started collecting some of my clothes and cash that I had stashed in the foam of the seats. I heard a big thud above me and then Shane lowered himself in. He looked at me and held his nose. We got what we needed and jumped back over the fence. We had to get the bus out of there. Each day that passed would cost us more to get it out of that impound.

Cash was starting to come our way from the professional "hanging out" we were doing, and I started putting it aside for the bus. Miraculously we managed to get the band together and rehearse a few times and even got to play the Whisky again, but the unity of the band was fractured and maybe some of us were just going through the motions. Either way, the show was not our best and it was a harsh reality that needed to be addressed. Chris got the band booked at a popular venue called Madame Wongs in Santa Monica. A funky punk rock Chinese restaurant, which turned out to be a really great gig. We didn't necessarily play very well, but we got a great response from the crowd. The scene there was more reminiscent of CBGBs in New York City in the late 70s, and we just seemed to fit in there more than the Whisky. Plus, we had some of our new friends come out for support and to party. Chris lent us the van so we could move our gear. We didn't see Mitch much between rehearsals and shows. We were pretty sure he was playing with some local cats and the girl he was hanging with got him a job at Guitar Center as a salesman. Mitch was settling into Hollywood, but Shane, Anthony, and I, not so much. I wanted to get back on the bus and return to Austin, reconnect with the management company and plug into the scene down there. I believed the rootsy element of the band would go over much better. Mitch was attracted to the flash and status that L.A. seemed to be cashing in at the time, but Anthony and Shane were grappling with the idea of starting a new life in a new place.

This trip made them realize they may not be ready for that kind of life change yet, and returning to New York was starting to pull on them. Even I was definitely Jonesing for some good pizza and bagels. The band was starting to split, and we all felt it. During a band meeting, Anthony and Shane brought up heading back to New York, so of course, I brought up getting the bus back and heading back to Austin. Mitch didn't say much, but after the meeting, he took me aside and said he wanted to meet me for lunch the next day at a pizza place he found that he thought I would like. That night, I did the rounds with Remi all over Hollywood, making deliveries and collecting cash. I slept in the next day, waking up with a hollow feeling in my gut. I got dressed, jumped on a bus, and made my way to the pizza place Mitch told me about.

John 'Sully' Sullivan

When I arrived, he was already there, which was strange because he was rarely on time for anything. It was a typical pizza parlor with yellow booth seats and tables that needed to be cleaned. I remember the place having no smell which is not a good sign. We ordered a few slices and sat down near the front window. Mitch jumped right into it. As I suspected, he was rehearsing with a local band. He felt something could really happen with them but that they lacked a great drummer. I knew then where the conversation would go. As I've mentioned before, Mitch had always heard me as a drummer more than anything else, and there was a chemistry we had that was different from what he had with Anthony. But hearing his words and his excitement mixed with the awful cardboard taste of that terrible pizza, I was pretty sure everything was about to fall apart. He also told me there was a position available at the guitar center and that I should go down there and meet the manager. Turns out the other members of the band he was playing with all worked at Guitar Center. And then he asked what I thought of the pizza. I lied.

THE BUS

The Guitar Center today is a shadow of its former self, but back in the 80s in Hollywood California, it was Mecca for guitar players, an equivalent to the world-famous Manny's Music in New York City. The large building is covered in murals of rock stars and has its own star-studded Hands of Fame impressed into the walkway of the entrance. A few days after meeting Mitch, I got on a bus and made my way down to the store. As I strolled in, I looked around until I saw him behind a counter. He waved me over. I almost didn't recognize him. He had on a button-down shirt and glasses, and his hair was pulled back in a ponytail. He nervously introduced me to several other employees and then the manager, who seemed like a nice guy. The sales positions wouldn't be available till next month, but he said they could use someone in the stockroom and for builds and setups and when the sales position became available, I would be offered it.

The feeling I had while listening to him was like I was floating outside of my body. I numbly agreed and shook his hand. He gave me some forms to fill out and told me to come back tomorrow morning to start my first day. I told Mitch I'd see him tomorrow and walked out. I felt like a zombie. My bones were telling me it was not the right thing to do, but I had no response. I just walked and walked until I was physically lost, and then I realized I was also spiritually lost as well. Even though the sky was blue and the sun was shining, inside me was complete darkness. I saw myself as a character in a Dostoevfsky or Beckett story caught in a cycle of absurdity and meaninglessness. I was missing something, something obvious, right in front of me, but I couldn't see it. When I returned to the apartment, I saw Anthony and Shane coming out of the liquor store below carrying a case of rolling rock, and we all went upstairs. Once inside, I told them I took a gig at Guitar Center that Mitch had hooked up. I could tell instantly that they thought I was planning to stay in L.A. by the way they both looked at each other. I said something like, "I might as well check it out; there may be some good connections there", but they knew it was bullshit. After our conversation, I threw my clothes in a bag and headed to the laundry mat so I would at least have some semi-clean clothes on my first day.

The next morning, I woke up extremely depressed, and my body felt broken from sleeping on the loveseat. Shane and Anthony were still passed out. We finished that entire case of rolling rock the night before. I took a shower, got dressed and went downstairs to catch the bus. It was like my body was on automatic pilot. I couldn't believe I was doing it. The bus ride and walking into the store was a blur. I don't remember if I even saw Mitch. The manager took me to the stock room and explained what needed to be done, but I couldn't concentrate on what he was saying, so I just nodded my head until he walked away and left me alone. I walked around the large stock room, just seeing what was there. I had no idea how long I did this, but eventually, I was knocked out of my trance by the sound of doors opening and the beeping of a truck backing up. Deliveries.

I ended up helping a couple of guys unload the truck of a few boxes. One of the dudes also worked in the stock room. He basically showed me how the numbers on boxes correlated to where they would be stored, but again, I was barely listening. He said after the boxes were put away, I could go to lunch. I stacked the boxes on a cart and rolled around the aisles, but because I didn't focus on what he was saying, I couldn't figure out where the merchandise was supposed to go. After a half hour, I gave up. I left the stock room and made a B-line for the front door. Once outside, I hung a right and started walking fast. I exhaled like I had been holding my breath the entire time I was inside, but then, out of nowhere, I stumbled upon a funky open-air diner that had a counter and old-school swivel stools.

I could smell the greasy burgers frying. "Wow, what a cool place" I thought, and grabbed a seat and ordered a burger and fries. I don't know how long I sat there, tormenting myself. I just knew I couldn't go back to that store. I paid the check and started walking back to the apartment. Years later, I would learn that little greasy spoon was the Sunset Grill, the namesake of Don Henley's song, and it was also one of the loneliest moments of my life. I had to snap out of it. Was the party over? Did I quit a nine-to-five job in New York only to get one in Los Angeles? I was pissed, mostly at myself. When I got to the apartment, no one was around. I walked down the hall to Remi's place and everyone was there hanging out. They all gave me a surprised look, and then, as if on cue, everyone started laughing. It was embarrassing. "That bad?" asked Shane. "Oh yeah!" I answered. They handed me a beer and a joint, and after that it was like nothing ever happened.

For those who have never witnessed a house party in the Hollywood hills during the 1980's, imagine a tribe made up of actors, models, directors, writers, producers, pornographers, agents, politicians, athletes, and rockstars and not a blue-collar plumber, or electrician in the bunch. We had to make the rounds with Remi, so we gathered up the powders, pills, and weed and headed to a big house party in the hills. This particular tribe ritualistically inhales copious amounts of legal and illegal substances. When our little posse of drugstore cowboys went as a group to the same party, each of us would take a section of the house or property and just hang out, roll a joint or chop up some lines, and then instantaneously we were open for business. Very quickly people would be buying whatever we were holding. In a matter of a few hours, we'd be cleaned out, and the party seemed to be just warming up. Remi wanted to head back to get more product and being that I wasn't in a festive mood, I went with him just to get some air.

On the way, he asked if I was ok. I must not have looked very well. "I have the perfect thing for you," he said with a hint of arrogance. When we arrived at his apartment, he rushed into the bedroom and came out holding a baggie of white powder. He opened it, poured the contents out onto one of the small hand-held mirrors on the coffee table and said, "Do a line of this; it's really good." He handed me the mirror with a straw, and without hesitating, I inhaled a pile of the stuff. "Eeeyaoowww", I winced, "what the fuck was that?" He said, matching my intensity, "That's crank, dude!". I thought I had inhaled pure poison. My entire sinuses became inflamed as water started pouring out of my eyes. "Crank?" I said, practically choking. "Yes, Crank!" He repeated. "Crystal, Meth, methamphetamine." Instantly, I felt sick. My whole body, from my skin to my organs to my bones, began rebelling against this horrible drug. "People like this shit?" I sputtered. "Come on," he said, "let's get back to the party." "No way, man," I said as I squeezed my nostrils together in pain and walked out his door, down the hall to my place fumbling for the keys to open the door.

Once inside, I went straight to the bathroom sink, desperately trying to rinse out the demon dust from my burning sinuses. Since I didn't close the apartment door, Remi popped his head in. "You gonna be, ok?" he asked sympathetically. "Yeah," I pronounced. "I'll see you later", and then he left, closing the door behind him. My whole head felt like it was on fire. I crawled onto the mattress, rolled onto my back and stared at the ceiling, begging some higher power to please not make the situation any worse, but of course it did. First, this horrible taste slithered down into my mouth, burning my throat. It was getting harder to breathe, like I was hyperventilating, and my heart started racing like it was going to jump out of my chest.

In my mind, I thought I was having a heart attack. I became paranoid and believed I was going to die alone in this sleazy Hollywood apartment. I had been lying there for hours, sweating and grinding my teeth, when Anthony and Shane came in. "Yo dude, are you ok?" they asked. I told them I thought I was dying. Back in the 80s, meth was more of a west coast thing, at least the illegal meth. In the late 60s and early 70s, doctors would add a very pure version of it to so-called vitamin drips for high-end clients, but for punks like us, meth was questionably synthesized in makeshift labs by rouge chemists called cooks, usually far away from populated areas because the process smelled so bad.

This version of Crystal Meth was a powerful stimulant and very toxic and probably mixed with something else like PCP. I laid on that bed, soaked in my own sweat, my mind reeling and my body frozen the entire night and most of the next day. After almost 12 hours of feeling like I was being crushed in a trash compactor, I finally started to come down, but I mean way down into the dark abyss of depression. I was drained and exhausted, and it felt like I was coming down with the flu. It was then that I realized I had to leave L.A. I had to get out of there. This partying, vagabond, bohemian life was going to kill me. At least that was what this mad, strange voice said in my head. Was I having a panic attack? It sure seemed like I was panicking. Shane and Anthony spent most of the time with me while I was tweaking, making sure I was ok. I told them about my intentions of leaving. They were relieved. With the three of us pooling our money together, we could get the bus out of the impound. The question then was, do we go back to Austin, Texas, or back to New York? All three of us were pretty confident that Mitch wouldn't leave L.A. Since we weren't a full band anymore, it probably would be wise to return to New York for reinforcements. At least, that's what we told ourselves. We talked about getting another guitarist and getting back on the bus and checking out Chicago, Cincinnati, Cleveland, and Kansas City instead of hunkering down in one city. It sounded good at the time.

BRING IT ON HOME

The next couple of days were about tying up loose ends, contacting the Whisky to get our gear, and preparing the bus for the almost three-thousand-mile drive back to New York. This is where we really needed Rick. There were numerous things to think about. First, we had to thank all the angels that took care of us and say our good byes. Then we had to tell Mitch. He stopped by the apartment to check in on us. We didn't get into details. We just wished him luck and said to keep in touch. I saw the strain on his face as he tried not to act surprised. And that was it. He walked out of the apartment and he was gone. We were not the best communicators. The following day, all three of us took the city bus to the impound and paid the thousand bucks to free our bus from vehicle prison. The damn bus only cost a hundred fifty.

As Shane drove us out of the impound, the bus seemed to be ok, but just in case, we took it to a garage for an oil change and checkup which took up most of the day. Handling the bus in urban environments was usually Rick's job, and it took a while to get used to it. We had multiple close calls. Afterwards, we drove to the apartment, loaded up our stuff, and then off to the supermarket, then the Whisky, and then the Rainbow. Getting the gear back on the bus seemed to drastically lower my anxiety. I felt complete again. It was unfortunate that Mitch and Rick weren't with us, but the three of us were focused and determined to escape the city. Folks hanging inside the Rainbow came out to see us off and wish us luck, and that was it. We turned around and headed back east. And then there were three.

We wanted to get out of the city as soon as possible and reorganize as soon as we were rural. We didn't want to chance any confrontations with Los Angeles law enforcement. Everything was moving so quickly that it was hard to focus on the city passing by us. We were fully focused on navigating and paying attention to the traffic. To avoid the bus dying out going through the mountains, we took a different route out of L.A. than getting in. My adrenaline was pumping. I didn't know if it was right to just up and leave, but the excitement of being free again and the wheels carrying me into the unknown was much better than what was going down on the streets of Hollywood. Slowly, the city evaporated behind us, and the landscape opened up, yellow and dusty. Cars poured in and out of the city like millions of ants from an ant hill. We came upon a truck stop and pulled in to make a plan.

There was shit all over the bus that was moving around, and it needed to be cleaned and packed correctly. Routes, timelines and who was driving, when and where, had to be calculated. All three of us were low on funds, so it would be best to make a B-line to New York. We guessed that if we took turns driving and sleeping, took limited breaks, and there were no dramas or interruptions, we could do it in three days. Sean volunteered to continue driving and take the first shift. Anthony and I cleared the couch and mattress in the back so we could both rest. On the dashboard, Shane poured out two rails of white powder from a baggie he retrieved from his pocket and deeply inhaled them both through a rolled-up bill and away we went.

The heat, the smell, and the noise all came rushing back as I lay on that couch that vibrated and jumped with every passing bump in the road. I doubted I could sleep without drinking, smoking, or popping a pill, but I wanted to stay sober. I needed to stay sober, to feel everything I was going through, intellectually and emotionally, but it wasn't easy. I could still feel the effects of the meth in my system, and I didn't like it. Eventually, after a couple of hours, I drifted into a sort of half-asleep, half-awake state, as if I was in the bus but not in my body. It was a strangely familiar feeling of peace that I recognized, but from where I didn't know. I snapped out of it when Shane pulled over for gas. We didn't fuss around. We relieved ourselves and got right back on the road. Shane drove through the night and into the morning till we eventually pulled over for some breakfast just outside of Phoenix. I couldn't believe how fast time was moving. Everything was passing by in a blur. After breakfast, we all took turns on a payphone calling back east, letting everyone know we were on our way home, a little older, a little wiser, and a whole lotta hungover.

Anthony took over after we left Texas, and then my shift started just outside Tennessee. After diving all night, we wound up somewhere in the hills of West Virginia just as the sun began to rise. This thick fog rolled in as big as clouds. We were on this tight country road with deep drop-offs on the sides, and I could barely see the road. I had to slow way down, but these giant eighteen-wheelers blew past us like rockets. Shane and Anthony were laying down and hadn't moved or said a word for hours. I tried calling out to see if they were just resting, but they were out cold. I figured let them be. It was pretty stressful, but just when I decided I should pull over, the fog seemed to roll back a bit so I kept going.

We came upon an old bridge, and just as I rolled onto it, a huge cloud rolled right in front of me. It took me by surprise, and I couldn't see anything at all. Then I heard a loud bang and the sound of crunching steel. I felt the bus fall over and things fall on top of me, but I still couldn't see out the window. I thought to myself, "Oh my God, we're falling off the bridge!" And then I shouted out loud, "Jesus!" I do not know what happened next, but for a moment, I thought I had died. I could still see the clouds, but I was no longer on the bus. I didn't know where I was, but wherever it was, I didn't feel alone there. Like my half-awake sleep earlier, I wasn't in my body, but this time, I sensed someone or something was there with me. Then I started to hear a faint sound like the wind that got incrementally pitched higher, louder, and faster until I felt this pull or push, and then all of a sudden, I was rushed back into my body and was sitting in the bus that was now partially pulled over on the side of the road with the bridge behind us and the engine still running. I was stunned. "What the hell just happened?" I said to no one. I quickly realized it wasn't the best place to be stopped, so I put it in gear a drove a few hundred feet till I came upon a side road and pulled over. I shut off the bus and stepped out alone and sat down on the wet grass. "What the hell just happened to me?" I thought to myself. Was I in shock? Did I fall asleep? I didn't feel the same. Something was different. Had I lost my mind? Was I dreaming? I had no idea how long I sat there, but eventually, Shane must have realized we weren't moving and got up and exited the bus. "Everything ok?" He asked groggily.

After a few beats of silence, I answered, "All good" "Just couldn't see because of the fog." But I definitely was not ok. Or was I? The rest of the way back was like a dream and at any moment, I thought, I would wake up. As we reached eastern New Jersey, the silhouette of the Manhattan skyline rose up in the windshield, like the Emerald City in The Wizard of Oz, and I knew I wasn't in Kansas anymore.

www.ingramcontent.com/pod-product-compliance
Lightning Source LLC
Chambersburg PA
CBHW051137120626
46547CB00012B/837